Forces of erosion are ever at work on the land. Mountains are pushed up by forces deep in the earth's crust, then gradually wear down under the attacks of rain and running water, of frost and wind-blown sand and glaciers. Rivers scatter their debris on the plains, and then patiently carve out valleys and gorges there. The atmosphere works its way into the crannies of rocks and soil, decomposing them bit by bit. Rocks are flaked or broken by sudden changes of temperature, and the soil heaves and sinks as its moisture freezes and melts. So long as the earth has its blanket of atmosphere, this war between the forces of building and forces of tearing down will go on.

To Anjou
with love from
Maureen & Evan
Jane & Kate
x x x

THE
WORLD
WE
LIVE IN

SPECIAL EDITION FOR YOUNG READERS

THE WORLD WE LIVE IN

By the Editorial Staff of LIFE and Lincoln Barnett
Text Especially Adapted by Jane Werner Watson
from the Original Version

LONDON   COLLINS   GLASGOW

Staghorn corals and a
school of **blue damselfish.**

ACKNOWLEDGMENTS

THE PUBLISHERS are grateful to the Editorial Staff of LIFE and Lincoln Barnett and to the many other persons as well as institutions that made THE WORLD WE LIVE IN possible—both in the book version and now in this special edition for young readers.

Since a complete list of all who made important contributions in the form of advice and information would occupy many pages of this book, the publishers must express appreciation to them as a group. The paintings were prepared by Rudolph Zallinger, Chesley Bonestell, Rudolf Freund, James Lewicki, Antonio Petruccelli, James Perry Wilson and Robert Gartland, Simon Greco, Walter Linsenmaier, and Richard Edes Harrison. Photographs were taken by Fritz Goro, Alfred Eisenstadt, Gjon Mili, Andreas Feininger, Loomis Dean, Roman Vishniak, J. R. Eyerman, and others to whom specific acknowledgments are made in the Picture Credits (page 212). This list also includes the names of individual copyright owners.

Delicate Arch, Utah

TABLE
OF
CONTENTS

PART I

THE EARTH IS BORN

THE WONDER OF IT ALL

ON SOME distant hilltop, perhaps half a million years ago, a man raised his eyes to the sky and wondered. In that moment mankind became human. Man began his ages-long search for truth, and left the other animals behind in the grand parade of life.

Early man's notion of the earth and the heavens remains a mystery to us. Perhaps he thought of land and sky somewhat as the ancient Egyptians did. For these people the world was an enormous room. The earth was its floor. The sky was a vast ceiling supported on four great columns and hung nightly by the gods with stars for lamps.

We can understand such notions. The earth does seem to stretch flat around us, toward the roll of the hills and the upsweep of the mountains. It seems very solid and motionless beneath our feet. Yet we know it is a round ball spinning through space, wrapped in a blanket of air. We know because we have been told. But is it not amazing that man ever figured it out?

Until a few hundred years ago most people still thought the world was flat, with terrible seas swirling around its edges and the sun moving over it each day. We know now that the earth is not the centre of the universe. It is one of the smaller satellites circling around a star which is our sun.

And our sun is not the centre of the universe. It is a rather second-rate star toward the outer fringe of a vast group of stars called our galaxy. We see this galaxy around us at night as a faint "mist" of thousands of stars. We call the densest part the Milky Way.

Moreover, our earth is not standing still. It is spinning on its own axis, like a top, at a speed of 1,000 miles an hour at the equator. It is whirling in an oval path around the sun at 20 miles per second. It is riding through space near the edge of the Milky Way at 170 miles per second. And as it whirls, it holds us to it with a strong pull called gravity.

Our earth is only a speck in the universe. But it is a very special part. For our earth is largely made up of forms of matter that are rare in the universe. The universe has stars as hot as 35,000,000°F. It has empty space as cold as −459.6°F. But our earth has just the right temperatures for rare and delicate forms of matter such as plants and animals. Most important to us, of course, is man, who can look at the world around him—from the tiniest living beings in a drop of water to the vastness of the universe—and marvel at its wonders.

A fiery cloud of cosmic gas and dust, somewhat like the swirling mass at the picture's centre, was probably the earth's beginning. Now in the stage shown by the large globe at the bottom, the earth will continue to change through ages to come.

The solar system may once have been a whirling cloud of gas and dust like this. Gravity and impacts of particles of light from surrounding space made tiny gas and dust particles drift together. Under increasing pressure, the cloud's centre grew hot and became our sun. Other lumps of matter in the cloud became planets and their moons. The long dark streaks in the picture are the planets' shadows.

IN THE BEGINNING

What was the beginning of the universe like?

About five billion years ago, most scientists believe, there were only clouds of gas and dust drifting in space. By the force of gravity and pressure of light from surrounding space, the bits of matter attracted each other and formed clusters. The clusters began to spin. And as they became thicker, their temperatures rose. At last they became stars. Some clusters of matter were in pairs or triplets and became double or triple stars. Some remained single, like our sun.

Our solar system at this time was an enormous, glowing disc. Within it, lumps formed, as in a pudding. The largest lump, at the centre, became our sun. As the millions of years passed, other large lumps became the planets, and smaller lumps their satellites, or moons. And some glowing lumps wandered in the system as comets.

THE CONTINENTS APPEAR

Around its orbit the fiery earth hurtled, century after century. The heaviest matter in the earth's bulk sank to the core, and the lightest rose to the surface. From inside the mass came great jets of water vapour, carbon dioxide, and other gases. Thus was formed the earth's atmosphere.

Slowly the crust of the earth cooled. For thousands—perhaps millions—of years, its heat was radiated out into space. Hot matter from inside

came bubbling up somewhat as water bubbles up in boiling. As this cooled, the heavier matter settled back into place, sealing the fiery heat in the centre of the planet. There it rages to this day.

So the centre of the earth is probably a gigantic ball of molten iron, 4,500 miles across. Its temperature of around 5,000°F. is about the same as on the surface of the sun. Around this iron core is the earth's great inner shell, the part that hardened first. Known as the "mantle," and perhaps 1,800 miles thick, it is probably made up of a heavy, grey-green, iron-rich rock.

Around this mantle lies the thin crust of the earth, no thicker than the skin of an apple compared to the fruit. The crust's under layer seems to be a shell of basalt, a black rock often found in lava. This shell, 10 to 20 miles thick, lines the oceans and forms the foundations of the land. Above this shell rise the granite continents on which we live.

These continents took shape amid the wildest of scenes. When the earth's surface was still hot, smoke and flame billowed out of it, and fiery fountains of molten rock shot up, spreading layers of lava over the land. Perhaps, where the crust below was weakest, these outpourings kept piling up until platforms of granite-like rocks stood up above the still-molten mass. Perhaps floating islands of lighter granite began to harden on the still-molten sea. Spreading outward and downward as more crystals were formed, they rested at last on the basalt basement. Or perhaps the granite gathered in great pools in the earth's crust and later, when it had hardened to stone, was pushed up above the heavier basalt by pressures from below.

No one knows for certain how those first continental blocks were formed, or how they found their present places. They may have hardened where they rest today. Perhaps they hardened in

In the fiery sea of molten rock that may have once covered the earth, hardening islands of granite could have formed our continents. The moon, still hot, was at this time only 10,000 miles away.

11

The **cooling earth** was long darkened by hot, dense clouds. As these cooled, they began dropping rain on the hot rocks below. This at first boiled off as steam. But as the rocks cooled, less and less of the rain boiled off. Instead, the water ran down into the hollows of the planet's surface and formed the oceans.

a single mass and then, under the force of the earth's rotation, separated and floated around the globe. This idea is suggested by the way the eastern coastlines of the Americas "fit" the coastlines of Europe and Africa. But most scientists think the continents have built up gradually, and are still being built as volcanoes pour out molten rock over the earth.

THE COMING OF THE WATERS

While the earth was still very hot, it was covered by dense clouds of gases. For perhaps thousands of years it lay dark, hot, and lifeless beneath those swirling clouds. Then, as the clouds grad-

ually cooled, some of the water vapour in them began to condense into drops and fall as rain. As the rain touched the hot rocks of the earth's surface, it boiled off as steam and rose into the dark, clouded atmosphere once more. But the earth's rocky crust continued to grow cooler. More and more water fell as rain, and less and less of it was boiled away by the earth's cooling rocky surface. The rain fell, harder and harder, perhaps for centuries. It fell on the high peaks of the young continents and into the valleys of the earth. Down over the rocks it poured, filling the low places with vast pools.

And when the rains began to slacken, and the clouds gradually thinned, the oceans glittered under the first earthly sunshine.

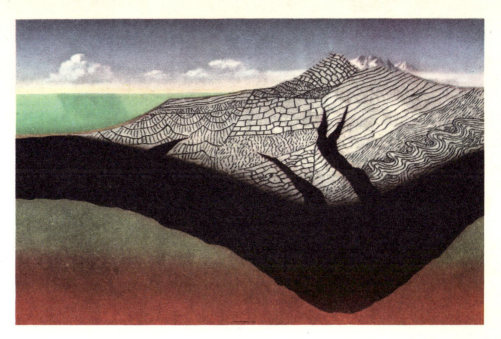

Earth's crust has two layers. The top layer is mostly granite. Below is basalt—a black, heavier rock. Mountain roots reach deep into the red-hot basalt of the earth's inner shell. In picture, basalt "fingers" running up into the granite are old lava-filled cracks.

Ages passed before the seas became what they are today. Since that first great flood, the level of the earth's waters has risen and fallen many times. Seas have rolled in over what is now dry land, and many places now under water have at other times been dry. Age after age, the outlines of the continents have changed.

THE BUILDING OF MOUNTAINS

As the earth's interior cooled, it probably shrank away from the outer crust. Like the skin of a drying apple, the earth's crust wrinkled, forming mountains and valleys. But as the mountains rose, falling rain and the gases in the atmosphere be-

gan to wear and eat them away. Over the centuries, mountain ridges and shoulders became furrowed. Deep canyons and valleys were carved along their lower slopes. And as the rain waters raged down the mountain-sides, they carried with them the minerals of the earth and its salts down to the sea—to make the salty sea we know. The wearing down of land by water has continued ever since.

How many mighty ranges of mountains rose up and were torn down when the earth was young no one can tell. Their roots lie hidden deep in the earth. But scientists believe there were at least ten great periods of mountain-building—periods when the earth's crust was actively shrinking around its interior.

Near the shore of a continent, forces in the earth (white arrows) make the crust crack, or fault. The sea floor sinks, and sediments (brown) pile up there. Next, sea floor and continent are crushed together and thrust up as mountains, which gradually erode away. Finally, a new fault occurs—and the story repeats.

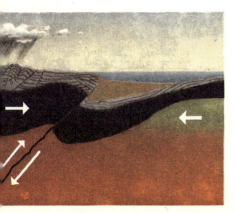  

As the earth's crust wrinkled, its rock cracked to depths of 350 miles. Along these cracks, called faults, rock masses would slide against one another. Often the great rock masses which are the continents pushed out over the lower ocean floor (as in the diagram at the bottom of page 13).

Sudden movements of the earth's crust brought earthquakes. Molten rock from deep inside the earth sometimes forced its way up through the cracks and, as lava, flowed out onto the land.

More than a billion years ago, hundreds of thousands of square miles of what is now eastern Canada were covered with molten rock. And the vast mountain chain of the Laurentians, now worn down to mere hills, was born.

Two hundred million years ago the Appalachian chain had already formed. From Newfoundland to Alabama stretched a line of peaks, perhaps snow-covered and as splendid as the Alps today. Erosion has long since worn them down.

The first landscapes took form slowly through uncounted millions of years. Great peaks and ranges were thrust up by the processes of mountain-building. As these arose, the falling rains began to wear them away. Canyons and valleys and gullies were dug. Erosion

All the high mountains of the earth as we know it—the Himalayas, Rockies, Alps, and Andes—were created within the last 60 million years. The Himalayas and some other mountain ranges are apparently still growing.

Scarcely one million years ago, the youngest of all mountains—the Cascades of the western United States—completed their rise from the sea with great volcanic bursts. And that period of mountain-building is still going on. All around the edges of the Pacific today are active volcanoes.

All of human history, back to the most primitive men of half a million or more years ago, has taken place during one brief period of mountain-building. The ranges that have been pushed up are high ones as mountain ranges go. And through their effects on such conditions as climate and vegetation, they have themselves greatly affected human history.

and mountain-building went on at the same time. Now and then, lava pushed up from the depths of the earth and spread in thick layers over the earth's crust. And at some point in this shadowy era, the first tiny beginnings of life appeared on the earth—probably in the sea.

Glaciers 4,000 feet or more thick, like the one at left, have scraped hilltops, rounded river and lake beds, scoured valley floors, crushed forests, and driven animal life to warmer regions. The great north polar ice cap, shown below, has been shrinking for the past 10,000 years.

THE MARCH OF GLACIERS

We live today in an age of glaciers. Both poles of the earth are covered by great ice caps. And wherever tall mountains rise, even in the tropics, snow and ice are seen.

It was not always so. Explorers in Greenland and Antarctica have found traces of plants and animals that can live only in warmer regions. These prove that long ago such areas were far warmer than they are today.

The earth has had several thousand-year-long ice ages. Great sheets of ice have grown and spread out from the poles, crushing forests and driving animal life toward warmer lands.

Glaciers may have many causes. New mountains rising up may block off air sweeping in from a warm ocean, so that land behind the mountains becomes cooler. Shifting of the earth's crust may change the directions of cold or warm ocean currents. The chemistry of the atmosphere may change. Volcanic ash in the air may block off part of the sun's rays. The sun may send out less heat, or the earth's position with respect to the sun may change.

The last great ice ages began about a million years ago. Glaciers covered more than one fourth of the earth's land surface. Over the United States they pushed south to where Louisville, Kentucky, now stands. Sheets of ice 2 miles thick covered New England, ground out the basins of the Great Lakes, and

The ocean floors were probably once flat plains of basalt lying 5 miles below the granite continents. Pressures inside the earth folded the plains into mountains and valleys. Volcanoes shot up lava, which sometimes formed islands. During the earth's great ice ages so much of the earth's water was frozen that the ocean level was lowered as much as 300 feet.

set the Mississippi and Missouri rivers on their present courses. As they moved southward, the ice sheets stripped soil from eastern Canada and carried it down over what is now the midwestern area of the United States. There the soil was dropped as the glaciers melted. Many a midwestern farmer today owes his bumper corn crop to a load of soil transported from a foreign country and conveniently dumped on his farm thousands of years ago.

At least four times the glaciers moved down and retreated again. The last advance ended about 10,000 years ago. The ice caps have now melted back as far as Greenland and the Antarctic continent, which are still capped by five million cubic miles of ice. The mountains of Alaska, New Zealand, and Scandinavia are still topped with glaciers. So are the higher Himalayas, Andes, and Alps. But the ice is retreating. In the Rockies and the Alps some glaciers have almost disappeared within the memory of living men. The ice packs of the Arctic and Antarctic are melting year by year.

The earth's climate may continue to grow warmer for several thousand years. As the polar ice caps melt, the seas will rise. If the caps melt away entirely, the ocean levels will rise by more than 100 feet—enough to cover New York, London, Paris, and many other coastal cities.

THE FUTURE OF THE EARTH

The earth is still young. It should last as long as our sun, and our sun should last for billions of years—unless some unlikely catastrophe takes place, such as a collision with another star. Perhaps 3 to 10 billion years from now its hydrogen will run low. Through long ages the sun may swell, slowly at first, then more rapidly. Fifteen billion years from now it may be, like some stars we know, a red giant many times its present size.

As the surface of the expanding sun nears the earth, all living things here will shrivel. The oceans will boil away and the heated atmosphere will be driven off into space. Red light will bathe the lifeless, scorched planet as it turns through countless centuries about the swelling sun.

Perhaps the earth will be swallowed up as the sun expands. If not, it may blossom into life again. For the sun will finally shrink, astronomers believe, as it once swelled. Temperatures on the earth will become mild again. But as the sun grows smaller it will shine ever more faintly. Eventually, 30 to 50 billion years from now, its last fires will flicker out forever. And unending night will rule in what was once our solar system.

But before this happens, the earth's great patterns will repeat themselves. Each day the rains and running waters will sweep 8 million tons of the land into the seas. All the towering peaks we know will crumble to the ocean floor, and new summits will rise. The earth's face will buckle and heave, volcanoes will roar, mountains will be pushed up. Glaciers will grind over plains and forests, and the seas will fall—later, as the millions of years follow one another, to rise again.

Foaming breakers pushed by an offshore wind batter a rocky beach along the California coast. An endless battle between sea and land goes on all over the world.

PART II

THE MIRACLE OF THE SEA

THE MIRACLE OF WATER

IF SOMEWHERE in space a viewer from another planet should examine our solar system, he might well name our planet Sea rather than Earth. For it is the great glistening sheath of water that covers very nearly three quarters of our globe that vividly sets it apart from the other planets circling our sun. More than any other physical feature of our earth, the sea makes it remarkably unique.

No other world within the range of man's vision has a sea. Mars has frost, some moisture, perhaps vegetation; but no sea. Mercury appears to have no water at all. Venus lies veiled behind dense clouds which, unlike the clouds of Earth, probably contain no water, nor even oxygen. The outer planets are too cold to have seas: Jupiter's surface is at 216°F. below zero, Saturn's at 240° below.

But our earth is nearly drowned in water. Only 29 per cent of its crust shows above the great ocean that hides the rest of the planet under a liquid layer averaging 2 miles in depth.

If all the land areas of earth—continents, islands, mountains—were somehow torn loose from their foundations and hurled into the sea, they would displace only one eighteenth of the water in the ocean basins. And if all the bumps on the earth's crust were smoothed down to an even sphere, the seas would flow about 8,000 feet deep all around the globe.

This water of ours has some properties all its own. Upon these depend our weather, our soil, and all living matter. For example, nearly all material substances expand when heated and contract when cooled (like the mercury in the thermometer). So does water, except that when it freezes it stops contracting and expands 9 per cent. This is why ice floats on lakes and rivers, and even on our salty seas, instead of sinking heavily to the bottom. If ice sank, especially in the seas, the cold seas of the earth would be frozen solid, save for a little melted ice on the surface; then the exchange of warm and cold currents could not continue—as it does now—to moderate the temperatures of the earth.

Water also can store great quantities of heat; so the oceans are reservoirs of heat from the sun, helping to keep the climates along their shores moderate.

Water dissolves more substances than any other liquid. Also, as water helps the process of erosion which is constantly washing away the high places of the earth, it sweeps minerals and salts, sand, silt, and soil from the land into the sea.

The Western Atlantic Basin is bounded by the Mid-Atlantic Ridge and the continental land masses. Deepest hollows are Cayman Trench (23,748 feet) and Puerto Rico Trench (28,200 feet). Note the volcanic island of Bermuda. By using the colour scale at right, one can compare the heights of land with the depths of the sea.

THE MIRACLE OF LIFE

Perhaps the most important fact about the sea is that it can remain liquid in the temperature range that prevails on Earth. Most of the matter in the universe seems to consist of flaming gases or frozen solids. The universe has a temperature range of millions of degrees. Only within a very narrow range can water remain in liquid form.

But Earth fortunately does supply that range.

Life as we know it also exists within that narrow temperature band. This should not cause surprise, for all living things not only use water but are largely made of it. The human body is about 70 percent water; and the chemical composition of man's blood is similar to that of sea water. The reason for this may be that life—as most scientists believe—originated in the sea.

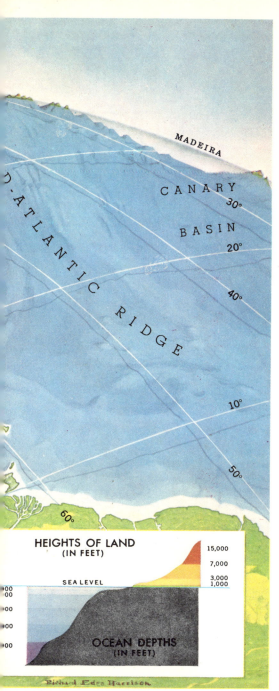

HEIGHTS OF LAND
(IN FEET)

15,000
7,000
SEA LEVEL
3,000
1,000

OCEAN DEPTHS
(IN FEET)

Richard Edes Harrison

The sweet waters of land, too, come from the salty sea. The great ocean basins of the planet hold some 300 million cubic miles of salt water. From this vast store 80,000 cubic miles of water are sucked up each year by evaporation—without salt—and then returned by rainfall. Much of this rain falls back into the seas; but more than 24,000 cubic miles of rain come down each year upon the continents. They refill the sweet-water lakes and streams, the springs and underground water tables, on which all the animals and plants depend for life. That is another of the miracles of our sea.

HOW THE SEA WAS BORN

When the planet was created, water vapour and other gases were held inside. As the inside began to cool and shrink, these gases were pushed out through volcanoes. They formed a thick cloud which, cooling, finally fell in a huge flood of rain. Probably this first flood did not supply more than 20 percent of the waters filling the oceans today. But for thousands of centuries afterward, as the earth continued to cool and to contract, new water was squeezed to the surface and some was spouted out into the oceans by underwater volcanoes. Maybe a billion years ago, the sea rose to its present level.

The Mid-Atlantic Ridge (at right) winds down the middle of the ocean, dividing it into several basins. Most of the ridge lies 9,000 feet below the surface, though its highest peaks emerge as islands. Because of its many arms, the Atlantic has more miles of coastline than the Pacific and Indian Oceans combined. This picture, in which shading indicates relative ocean depths, makes clear that the ocean is actually a landscape under water. Like dry land it has mountains, plateaux, valleys.

The **Countless Islands of the Pacific** are barely suggested in this over-all view. The Pacific covers nearly half the earth, from the North Polar Sea to the Antarctic. Ridges on the ocean floor in some places emerge as series of islands. Deep trenches and hundreds of lofty undersea mountains also are found. Below Alaska rises one of the longest, highest cliffs on earth. The large land area at left is Australia; at top left is the mainland of Asia, and at right are the continents of North and South America.

SEASCAPES

Really there is one limitless ocean circling the planet. Between the Antarctic continent and the tips of South America and South Africa, a ship could sail round and round the earth forever without ever sighting land.

Some geographers call this water ring the Antarctic Ocean. Northward where the continents divide the sea, geographers have named one section the Atlantic, one the Pacific, one the Indian Ocean. The Arctic or North Polar Sea is usually counted as part of the Atlantic.

It is only since 1920 that men have had a picture of the undersea landscapes. In 1920 men learned to measure the depth of water by the time it took for a sound impulse to travel to the bottom and back. These sonic soundings were soon taken in great numbers. They were charted on hydrographic charts. And from these charts men could map the dark, unseen depths and gain a picture of that strange, lightless, undersea world.

As on land, there are mountain ranges, volcanoes, cliffs, plateaux and plains under the sea. There are valleys and deep gorges. But many mountains are higher, many ranges are longer, many canyons and gorges deeper, than on the surface. If Earth's highest mountain peak, Mt. Everest (29,002 feet), were dropped into the deepest part of the ocean, water a mile deep would still flow above it.

There are other differences. The undersea mountains have no erosion—no wearing away by wind, rain, and stream. The cover of the sea protects its mountains from wear. Only the loftiest peaks, which rise above the surface as islands, are attacked by wind, surf, and rain.

Each ocean has three main sections: the continental shelves, the continental slopes, and the deep-sea floor. The shelves are part of the block of the continent. In some ages they have been above water, in others they have been flooded. These shelves slope outward from the shore for 10 to 200 miles. The water may be 200 to 600 feet deep before the great block of the continent drops away in steep slopes, often plunging down to depths of 12,000 feet and forming loftier cliffs

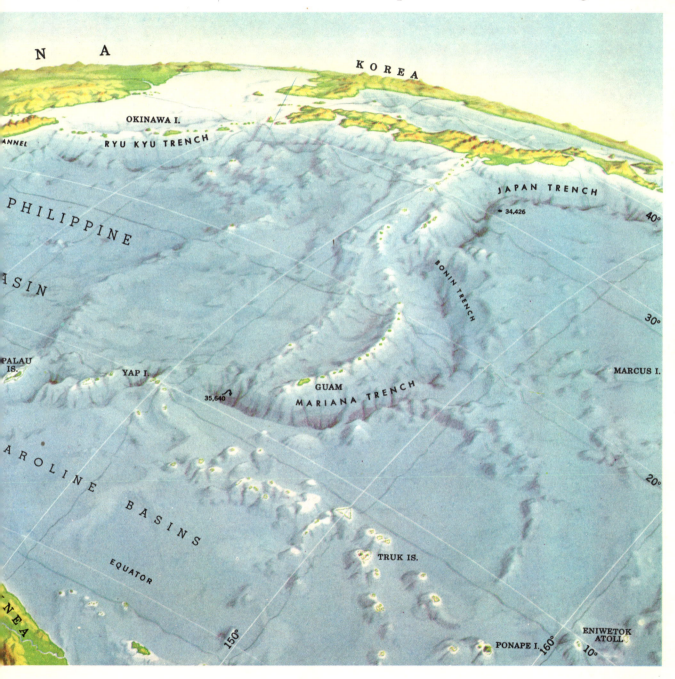

The **Southwest Pacific** has undersea outlines which are the most rugged on earth. Earth's deepest abysses are the Philippine Trench (34,440 feet) and Mariana Trench (35,640 feet). The Mariana Islands (including Guam) top a 500-mile range of undersea volcanic mountains.

An Atlantic seascape. Here the mountains and cliffs of the ocean bottom appear as we might see them if the waters were drained away. The dotted line indicates the ocean's surface. At left is the gently sloping continental shelf of eastern United States, covered with greenish

than any ever seen by man. And where the sea floor has sunk sharply, the total depth of such drops may reach 30,000 feet—1,000 feet deeper than Mt. Everest is high.

The faces of these great ramparts are not smooth; they are cut by deep canyons, reaching far back into the continental block. In the Atlantic between Bermuda and the Azores scientists have discovered a system of channels as vast as the Mississippi and all the rivers that feed it—a system which may begin with the deep canyons known to exist off Greenland. One such canyon continues the course of the Hudson River 150 miles out into the Atlantic Ocean. A 145-mile-long canyon has been located at the mouth of the Congo River in Africa.

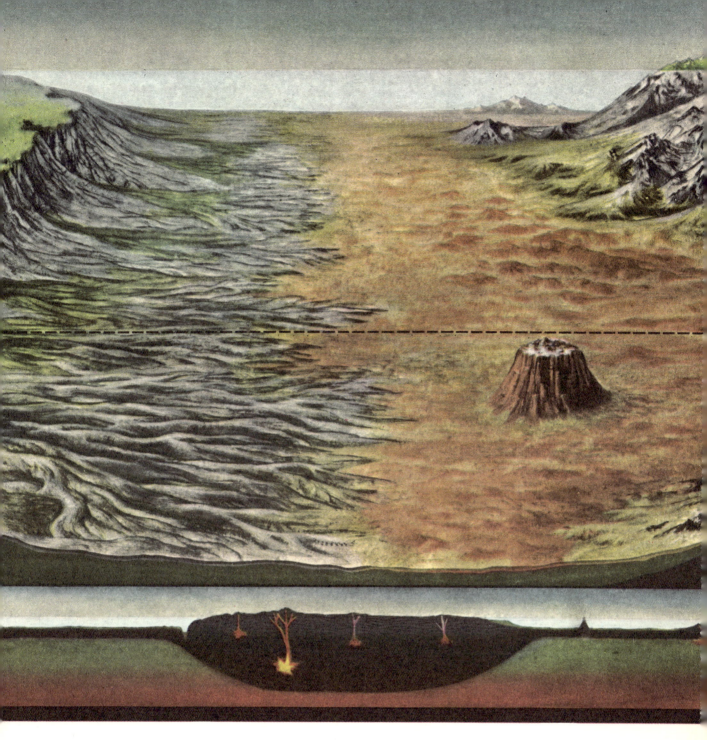

sediments. From this the furrowed continental slope plunges 16,000 feet to the ocean floor. Rising from the floor, at right, are ooze-mantled mountain peaks of the gigantic Mid-Atlantic Ridge; also a white-topped coral atoll and deep-rooted volcanic islands. Long

Perhaps some canyons were cut by streams when the continents were higher above sea level. However, some canyons are at depths of 3 miles. Scientists doubt that the sea has risen that much. The causes of the deep-water canyons and some others may be submarine earthquakes, faults, underwater currents, or landslides of mud down from the continental shelves.

At the foot of the continental slopes, lying in the darkness and cold under miles of water, is the deep ocean floor, measuring half the total surface of our planet. It is far from a wholly flat floor. This ocean bed is seamed and ribbed with deep trenches and high mountain ranges. It is carpeted with layers of sediment, averaging half a mile in depth.

inset picture (lower left) shows that continental block actually extends far out beneath ocean waters. The rocky ocean floor lies under about 2,000 feet of varicoloured clays and marine ooze. The heights of mountains, volcanic islands, and continent here are exaggerated.

In the deep ocean basins this sediment is not made up of coarse sand, silt, and mud washed down from the land and rivers by rain. Those lie closer to shore. Here in the depths the sea floor is covered with finer fabric: red clay from the continents, and undersea oozes—pink, white, yellow, red, green, brown. These are the remains of countless tiny sea creatures whose shells or skeletons have drifted down from above, century after century, in numbers so vast as to be meaningless to man. (These sea animals are described in Chapter VII, CREATURES OF THE SEA.) There are also fragments of lava and pumice spewed out by undersea volcanoes, and some minerals which appear to be remains of meteorites from outer space.

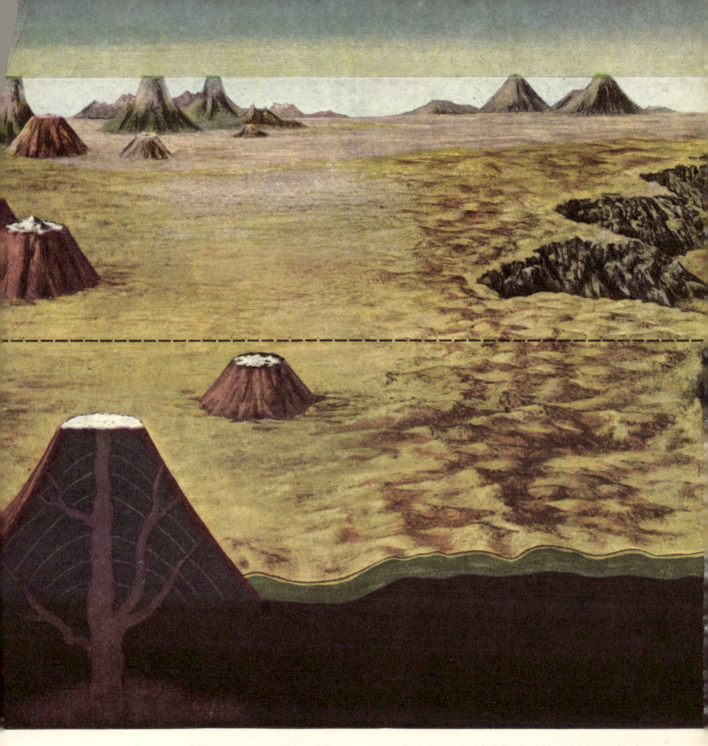

A Pacific seascape. At far left are a group of sunken volcanic islands and undersea volcanoes with their tips showing above the surface. At left, front, are several Guyots, sunken islands, with coral tops. More to the right lies a typical oceanic trench, 5 miles deep, with sediments

UNDERSEA MOUNTAINS

Most curious and wonderful of the unseen vistas of the sea are the great mountain ranges. Their peaks—treeless, snowless, sunless—rise in darkness, save where the tallest peaks break the surface of the ocean and appear as islands.

The greatest range is the Mid-Atlantic Ridge, which winds down the middle of the Atlantic Ocean from Iceland almost to Antarctica. This mightiest range on earth is 10,000 miles long, 500 miles wide. Most of its peaks lie a mile or more beneath the surface. But a few of them appear as the scattered islands of the Atlantic. Highest of the peaks, Mt. Pico of the Azores towers 7,613 feet above the surface of the sea and

FOLD OUT—DO NOT TEAR

gathering miles thick at the bottom. At the middle of the picture, steep continental slopes are shown carved into great gullies and canyons. The continental shelf, much grooved and furrowed, leads gradually to the Pacific coast of the North American continent. At far right,

plunges 20,000 feet below the surface to the sea floor.

The Hawaiian volcano Mauna Kea is the highest mountain on earth, rising about 31,000 feet directly from the Pacific floor, though only its final 13,823 feet appear above the sea.

Almost all mid-ocean islands are volcanic, as are most of the mountains of the sea. It seems

that great cracks opened in the ocean floor. And through these long cracks molten rock welled up to build the vast ocean ranges.

One strange type of volcanic undersea mountain is called a "Guyot." Guyots are flat-topped volcanoes whose tops were apparently cut off at sea level by the action of the waves some time long ago when they stood above water. Yet now

the artist has painted in the coastal mountain range and a canyon on the scale of the Grand Canyon of Arizona. These look like mere hills and gullies when they are compared to the majestic mountain and canyon scenery hidden in the dark, cold depths of the sea.

some lie more than half a mile below the surface. More than 500 have been located in the Pacific Ocean, and a few in the Atlantic also. Perhaps they sank from their own weight or because of some collapse of the ocean floor.

As there are valleys on land, so there are valleys under the sea. These great oceanic valleys, called trenches, plunge as deep as 35,000 feet below the ocean surface—a much greater distance than any land mountain rises above sea level.

Oddly enough, these trenches are found near continental slopes or near chains of islands. The reason may be that as mountains are thrust up, great deeps are formed to balance them. Century after century, sediments pile up—layer on layer, perhaps mile on mile—in these troughs. The

Atlantic currents. Warm currents are shown in red, cold in blue. Along the equator (below middle of map) currents move east to west, then curve around to the north and south. Most important is the Gulf Stream, flowing up past Florida, then across the Atlantic, warming the British Isles and coastlines farther north.

ocean's floor may some day buckle here, thrusting the mass of hardened sediment up to form new mountain ranges.

This has happened in past ages, and it can happen again.

These deepest spots of the ocean may be new land masses in the making for future ages. There they lie in watery darkness, these rich scenes which no man's eye has ever looked upon. As long as there is water in the oceans, man will probably never reach those depths, except by mechanical devices not yet invented. In the ocean deeps the pressure of the water is 7 tons per square inch.

THE CIRCLING CURRENTS

The forces that keep the ocean waters in motion, sending warm waters toward the poles and cold waters to the tropics, are three: wind, rotation of the earth, and changes in density of the water.

Steady winds directed by the rotation of the earth are the Trade Winds from the east. Just above the equator they blow out of the northeast; just below the equator they blow out of the southeast. They drive the great westward-rolling Equatorial Currents. As these currents near continents, they swing southward in the Southern Hemisphere and circle about, speeded on their

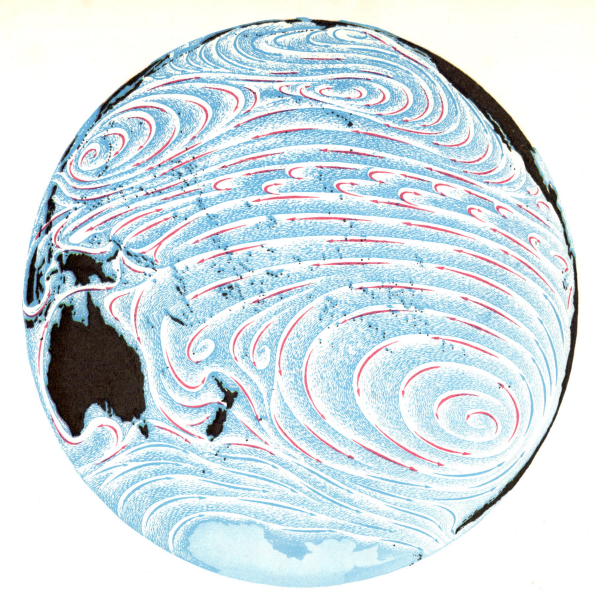

Pacific currents. Along the equator, main currents move east to west, as in the Atlantic. To the coasts of Peru (far right) they bring cold waters from the far south. From the north they bring cold waters down along California (upper far right). Another current circles up to warm the islands of Japan (upper far left).

circular route by the chilly Westerlies. They swing northward in the Northern Hemisphere and circle in the same way.

These currents deeply affect the climate of the lands they touch. Most famous is the North Atlantic current known as the Gulf Stream. It sweeps across from Florida toward Norway in several streams. At its maximum speed of 6 miles an hour, it may carry 1,200 times as much water as the Mississippi River.

Some currents are caused by the fact that when water is cooled, it becomes denser—that is, heavier. This heavier water tends to sink down and move under warmer, lighter water.

The density of water also depends on the amount of salt dissolved in it. Fresh water is lighter than salt water; thus rainfall over a certain part of the ocean will make the water there less salty and therefore lighter than it is elsewhere.

A famous density current is found at the gateway to the Mediterranean Sea. Over this sea little rain occurs, and much evaporation by sunlight, so the water is more salty and dense than in the Atlantic. At Gibraltar the Mediterranean water sinks and moves out into the Atlantic, while above it the lighter Atlantic water flows into the Mediterranean.

full moon or new moon — there are the high "spring" tides. When sun and moon pull in different directions—at the first and third quarters—there are the lower "neap" tides.

The moon revolves around the earth, from west to east, completing the trip in about 29 days. High and low tide therefore occur—during most of the year—about 50 minutes later each day.

Tides are influenced by the sizes, shapes, and depths of ocean basins. In each basin the waters tend to slosh back and forth like water in a pail you are carrying. These sloshings may work with or against the tide. In some places, like Tahiti or Nantucket, the tide lifts only a foot. But at Nova Scotia's Bay of Fundy, which is like a funnel, it surges up 40 feet. Twice a day 3,680 billion cubic feet of water rush in and out of this funnel, producing the highest tides in the world.

High tide. Six hours after low tide the seas surround the walls of the famous abbey. The very gradual slope of the shore is the reason why the tide covers so large an area.

Low tide. Mont-Saint-Michel, off the coast of France, at low tide is surrounded by 11 square miles of sand and mud flats. Later the tide comes in at the speed of a fast walk.

THE PULSE OF THE TIDES

The gravity which holds the waters to the earth and keeps them from whirling off into space is the same force that causes tides.

The ocean waters are attracted toward the moon by gravity. When the moon is overhead, the waters bulge out toward it, and there is a similar bulge on the opposite side of the earth. At its highest the bulge is known as high tide along the shores. Low tide comes when the moon is at the horizon.

The sun also exerts some pull on the waters, though not so much as the much closer moon. When sun, moon, and earth are all in line—at

THE RESTLESS WAVES

Most people think of a "wave" as meaning any vertical rise or swelling of the sea. Actually there are three types of waves.

When a wave first forms in wind-blown water, it is called a sea. When it has left the storm area and is travelling across calm water, it is a "swell." When it reaches land and breaks, it is "surf."

The height of a storm wave, or sea, depends on violence of the wind, length of time the storm lasts, and extent of open water over which the storm rages. Most seas are only 5 to 12 feet high, but a two-day storm may produce 20-foot waves. Even 50-foot waves have been reported.

Each drop of water in a wave moves in a circular pattern, as if on a wheel. For a drop near the surface this circle is the height of the wave; deeper down the circle is smaller. Any one drop of water moves ahead at only 1 to 2 percent of the speed of the wave. At about 600 feet or more below the surface, the sea is always calm.

Swells travel under their own momentum across wide areas of windless water. They are low, widely spaced, and fast-moving. They keep travelling in an orderly pattern to far-distant

An ocean wave, after a journey of perhaps hundreds of miles. curls forward and falls thundering along the sands.

shores. As they travel, their height lessens, the spacing between waves lengthens, and their speed increases. Eventually a swell may travel faster than the wind that set it in motion.

When it nears a shore, the wave "feels bottom." Slowed by friction against the sea bottom, it rises from a low swell to a narrow, steep crest. The crest hurries forward faster than the slowed-down wave. Breaking into foam, it tumbles forward in a burst of fury on to the sand.

Crescent beach. The waves cut into weaker stretches in the rock cliffs on England's south coast. For centuries they have been cutting these coves and depositing sand in them.

Along jagged coastlines—like these at Land's End, England —the sea is gradually wearing down ancient rocky cliffs.

Chisels of the sea (right) cut rock into strange forms. Weaker parts of rock formations are worn away first, leaving the stronger parts in the form of sea caves, arches, and lonely columns. These are formations off the Oregon coast.

THE SEA AS A SCULPTOR

The power contained in a breaking wave is tremendous. A wave may strike the shore with a force equal to the pressure of 6,000 pounds per square foot. These waves can hollow out or pull down rock cliffs. In some parts of the British Isles they are eating away the coast at the rate of 15 feet a year.

Storm waves tend to tear down the shores. Gentle waves are the builders, for they may leave numberless grains of sand against offshore bars to build up new beaches.

Behind these new sheltering sand bars, tidal marshes grow up. They are built of sediment left by waves and washed down from the land by streams.

Miles of new land like this are built along shorelines where the land has been lifted up so that a gentle slope of the continental shelf is now above water. There are many such beaches along the southeastern United States. For every cliff that crumbles under the hammering of the sea, somewhere a new beach is being built, a new coral reef is growing, or a new volcanic island being thrust up.

The sea and its shores are ever changing. As glaciers grow or melt, they greatly change the amount of water in the seas. Earthquakes change the shapes of ocean basins. There was a time when much of North America was covered by sea. At other periods Alaska and Siberia were joined by a land bridge, and most of the East Indies were a part of Asia—so high did the land masses rise.

There will be other changes in the future which we cannot foresee. We can only be sure that through the ages the sea will continue its miraculous labour.

Wave-built beach. The ocean waves, slowly piling up the sand, have built many miles of long beaches like this.

PART III

THE FACE OF THE LAND

CONSTANT CHANGE

"There is nothing constant in the universe,
All ebb and flow. . . ."

So SPOKE the Roman poet Ovid 2,000 years ago. Certainly he was right about old Mother Earth, for she is always changing.

Every hill and highland—every cliff, crag, and rock—is being eaten away by rain, frost, wind, and ice. And in time the mightiest mountains will be levelled and washed away into the sea. But this does not mean the earth's surface will some day be flat. For every mountain that is worn and washed away, a new one comes into being. Immense forces of lifting up as well as wearing down are ever at work on every inch of the earth's surface.

The forces of uplift start deep inside the planet. They cause the earth's crust to buckle and bend upward, from time to time. This buckling creates highlands, plateaux, and mountain ranges.

The forces of the atmosphere also keep working. Wind and water are constantly rubbing and scraping and dissolving away the earth's high places. They blow or float powdered rock and soil down from the heights to the valleys and the sea.

Together these forces of upbuilding and down-tearing have shaped and re-shaped the face of our planet since its earliest days.

In some areas the forces of building seem busiest today. Here the land is shaken by earthquakes; volcanoes pour out masses of molten lava, cinders, and ash, building new mountain peaks in a few months or years. Here, too, other mountains may be very slowly taking form—some by bulging and folding of the earth's crust, some by cracking of the crust and the rising of great blocks of surface rock along these cracks.

Sharp, sudden shiftings in the earth's surface are called earthquakes. They are commonest today around the rim of the Pacific Ocean, but they can happen—and have happened—elsewhere, too. The rock crust suddenly moves along lines of weakness called "faults." Sometimes the shifting is sideways. For example, in the San Francisco earthquake of 1906, for 200 miles along the line of weakness (called the San Andreas Fault) roads and fences

A folded mountain. Millions of years ago, a sea covered this area. Layers of sediments— remains of sea life and materials washed from the land—formed on the sea bottom. Tremendous forces inside the earth pressed upward slowly against this sea bed until it arched up in a tremendous dome far higher than this mountain shown. Meanwhile the forces of destruction went to work. Wind, frost, and rain wore away the top and sides of the dome. Today the long rocky spine is exposed. The surrounding ridges are all that remains of other layers that once arched over the top. This is Sheep Mountain on Wyoming's Big Horn River.

39

A volcanic mountain. Deep in the earth, molten rock bubbled and surged, seeking a way out. Where it found cracks in the rocks, the lava pushed into them. At last it found its way to the surface, flowed out, and piled up, building a mountain called a volcano, with a cone at its centre through which hot gases, cinders, and rock could still find their way up. The mountain at left, Mt. Hood in Oregon, is volcanic. It is either extinct (lifeless) or dormant (sleeping). It has not exploded for many, many years. But from its form we can say that it was built up partly from quiet flows of molten lava and partly from noisy outbursts of cinders and rock chunks. Lava flows alone usually will form a mountain of a more evenly rounded shape.

were broken and wrenched out of line by as much as 21 feet.

Along this line of weakness there is still an uneasy shifting of two inches a year. Sometimes, instead, the shifting is up and down. In the great Alaska earthquake of 1899, a section of the coast was lifted nearly 50 feet.

In areas that are being lifted up, you see rocks freshly tilted and askew. Mountains are high, sharp-peaked, and slanting steeply upward toward the sky.

Where forces of destruction have had their way, the landscape wears a different face. Rain, melting snows, wind, and glaciers through long ages have worn, gullied, sand-blasted, scraped, and bulldozed off the once-towering mountain peaks. Now the land has plains, low rounded hills, and broad valleys, down which streams like the quiet old Mississippi wander to the sea.

HOW MOUNTAINS ARE BORN

The three principal types of mountains are the volcanic, block, and folded types.

Most volcanic mountains (see above) look like what they are—enormous heaps of hardened lava and ash. An even flow of lava usually forms a smooth, evenly rounded, cone-shaped mountain. The earth today has more than 500 active volcanoes and several thousand which are either extinct or dormant.

Traces of long-vanished volcanoes are seen here and there. Crater Lake in Oregon may be the wreck of an ancient exploded volcano. Lonely rock towers in deserts of Arizona and New Mexico are the necks of old volcanoes whose outer slopes have been worn away.

Here and there we find long ridges of igneous rock. This is rock that was once molten. It flowed

A block mountain. Ages ago a section of the earth's crust cracked away from the rock around it and was shoved sharply upward to form this mountain (near Las Vegas, Nevada). Layers of rock which once lay neatly on top of one another now slant sharply. The face of the mountain has been scarred by ages of erosion.

out through volcanoes, came up through cracks in the earth, or spread out under rock layers which have since worn away.

Sometimes lava pushed up under the earth's crust like a huge bubble and so made a rounded hill or mountain.

But most mountains are not volcanic. Many rose up when the earth's crust was pushed or bent so hard by forces from below that it broke. Sometimes the breaks are hundreds of miles long. They are called faults.

As the sides of the break pushed against each other, one side was forced up in one terrible, grinding shiver. Cliffs formed in this way are called fault scarps or escarpments. A series of these movements may build up whole ranges of so-called fault-block mountains (above).

The Sierra Nevada of California are a single tilted block 400 miles long and 60 miles wide. The once-level top is now the gentle western slope. The eastern wall, lifted up by repeated movements, is a gigantic fault scarp over 2 miles high. These are young mountains, and they are probably still growing.

Most great mountain chains of the world—the Alps, Andes, and Rockies—are not simple fault-block mountains but folded mountains. On page 38 is an extraordinary photograph of a folded mountain. Such mountains formed when the rocks

were slowly pushed up until they buckled into ridges like sea waves.

Most folded mountains were perhaps once part of great sea bottoms. In a broad hollow of rock, age after age, remains of tiny sea animals, as well as powdered rock washed in from the land, piled up in layers hundreds and thousands of feet thick. Under this huge weight the rock crust below sank slowly, but huge pressures from the sides at last buckled it up. The hardened sediments are known as sedimentary rock.

The Appalachian Mountains are old folded mountains. They have layers of sediment in some places 6 or 7 miles thick. In the great sea which once extended from Newfoundland to the Gulf of Mexico, sediments collected for nearly 300 million years before the final great upheaval that raised the Appalachians.

An ancient sea bottom. This cross section shows how sedimentary rocks overlying the basic rock (in red) may be folded into mountains, then worn down to gentle hills.

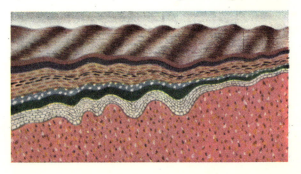

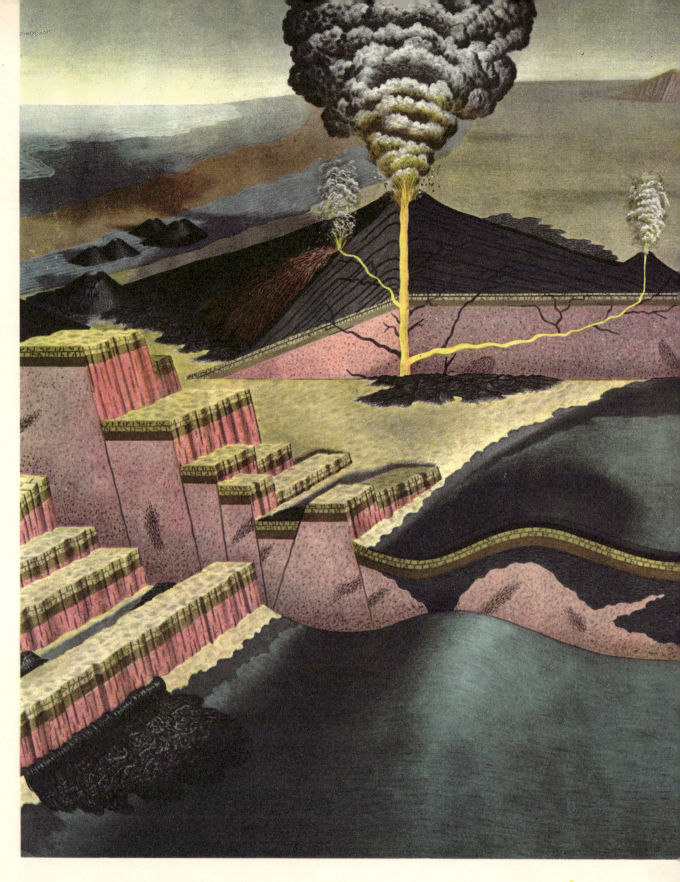

Forces of uplift. From deep in the earth, forces shape the face of the land by causing the crustal rocks to break and fold into highlands, hills, and mountain chains. This picture shows no real landscape, but rather the way an imaginary section of the earth might look with all soil and plant life stripped away and with all the forces of uplift at work on the bare rocks. The three principal mountain types—block, volcanic, and folded—are shown from left to right as they might appear had wind, rain, and streams not gone to work on them. In the left front are block mountains formed by the uplift of broken sections of crust rock.

Under them to their right, lava can be seen pushing out. Behind them, at left, are several cinder cones—heaps of volcanic ash that has blown out of holes in the earth's crust. Farther right is an active volcano in cross section, producing smoke, ash, and lava. To the right of the volcano you can see the formation known as a laccolith, formed when a layer of rock was pushed up like a bubble by lava from below. In the foreground the earth's crust has wrinkled to form a range of folded mountains similar to the Appalachians. Behind, at right, is a tilted block mountain. Its steep face rises along the fault line; its back slope is gentle.

Rain, wind, and streams working through old limestone have produced these rock spires in Utah's Bryce Canyon. Water has both dissolved and scraped away the rock. Weaker layers have been worn deepest.

HOW MOUNTAINS ARE WORN AWAY

As soon as new mountains start rising, the never-ending forces of erosion start tearing them down.

First comes weathering. The atmosphere is the chief weathering agent. This usually invisible blanket of oxygen, carbon dioxide, and **water vapour** which covers the earth can seep into the smallest openings in rocks and there do its destructive work.

Elements in the atmosphere combine chemically with elements in the rocks and cause the rocks to crumble and decay. Water dissolves parts of rocks. Where plant life has been growing, acids from old, decaying plants speed the crumbling of rocks to form soil. The roots of growing plants also force their way into cracks and, by gradual pressure, force rocks apart.

In cool climates, frost is a most important worker. Water seeps into cracks in the rock during the warmth of the day. At night it freezes; and, in freezing, water expands 9 percent. The force of this expansion can split small stones or pry away great slabs of rock from the face of cliffs.

As soon as bits of rock have been loosened by weathering, water and gravity start to carry them away. Gravity is the basic force. It is gravity (which draws everything toward the centre of the earth) aided by water, ice, and wind that causes the soil on slopes and hillsides everywhere to keep moving continually downhill.

Occasionally a cliff collapses, a landslide carries tons of soil down a steep slope, or a great mudflow or rockfall occurs. But even on slopes thickly covered with plants and trees, the whole blanket of soil is moving, all unseen, ever so slowly but steadily downward.

All these forces strive to level the land wherever it has been thrust up. Rain falling on fault-block mountains carries the softest particles of the rock with it, hollowing out small grooves. These grooves grow into deep V-shaped canyons. After some ages, there are no flat tops left on the blocks. They have all been carved into ridges and furrows. Even volcanic slopes are worn away.

Down the slopes of the folded mountains, too, water finds the easy path and digs them deep. And between the ridges or great folds wider streams cut their way toward the sea.

A level plain in cross section shows remains (left) of folded mountains worn down by centuries of erosion. At far right, an old underground lava flow is now exposed as a ridge.

Stream erosion. The swift-flowing Yellowstone River in Wyoming once ran along the surface at the level of the rocks at the top of this picture. Below the river was hard volcanic rock. But the river, eating away at this hard rock for about 150,000 years, has worked its way down 740 to 1,200 feet. This is a perfect example of stream erosion. The swift young Colorado River has taken about a million years to carve the Grand Canyon a mile deep and 8 miles wide at the rim. During that same million years the slow-moving old Mississippi River has washed away only about 150 feet of rock from its whole broad basin.

HOW WATER SHAPES THE LAND

Water is the great leveller. If you watch drops of water falling on soil, you will see that each drop acts as a miniature bomb. It blasts a tiny crater in the ground where it strikes.

This action of the raindrops is the first step in the wearing down of the land. Then the raindrops gather in low pockets and push downhill toward brooks; the brooks join larger streams; the streams flow into rivers. And the rivers cut channels to the sea.

The earth receives an average of 28½ inches of rain each year. Some desert areas, like Death Valley, have as little as 2 inches a year. Some water-soaked jungles, as on the slopes of the Himalayas, receive 450 inches a year.

Some rain water soaks into the ground. Some returns quickly to the skies through evaporation. But most of it—enough to fill a gigantic box 30 miles wide, 30 miles long, and 10 miles deep—runs off the land into the seas each year. And as it runs down to the sea—from which some of it will be evaporated into the atmosphere again—all this water carries with it bits of the land.

Over the years, stream erosion does more land-levelling than all other kinds of erosion together. Not only does running water wash away rock fragments, but these fragments act as tiny scrapers. They scoop out hollows, cut away banks, and help enlarge the channel of the stream while it is carrying them away.

A stream's power to destroy rock is increased when it carries more water and runs faster. A stream filled by a flood and flowing ten times as fast as usual may wear away many, many times the usual amount of rock.

The steepness of the grade down which it runs controls a stream's power. The steepest grade of all is a waterfall. And the plunge over a waterfall gives a stream very great power.

The waters roaring over the brink of Niagara Falls plunge down into the pool below at 50 miles an hour. They continually deepen and widen the pool, undercutting the cliffs above. From time to time, chunks of rock tumble down from the lofty brink of the falls. Thus the falls gradually move back. By cutting away their rocky bed at the rate of 3½ feet a year, these falls have moved upstream 7 miles from their original location.

Swift young streams cut almost straight downward. They form steep V-shaped valleys (page 46). But as time goes on, the sides of the valley become worn, and little by little the channel widens. When the river is old, like the Mississippi, it winds slowly down a broad quiet valley.

An alluvial fan. Mountain streams, swollen by rains, have brought down sediments from the high country and spread them out here like a great grey fan in California's Death Valley.

Wind-eroded arch. Water seeping through the soft rock first weakened this Utah sandstone. Then came the wind, which whirled sand against the rock and rubbed it away grain by grain. At long last the wind tunnelled through.

Wind-eroded soil. Wind has swept away the soil from the roots of these Death Valley "arrow weeds." Now the roots reach downward through empty air.

THE WORK OF WIND

In dry areas, wind is a powerful force in erosion. Carrying billions of particles of loose rock, the wind like a giant sand-blasting machine hurls them against the hills and cliffs, sometimes carving out strange arches and towers.

Wind blows away loose soil, leaving some desert areas floored with bare rock rather than with sand. It has even, in some places, scooped out hollows miles square and hundreds of feet deep.

Sand dunes. Rocks on the mountains bordering Death Valley have been weathering for thousands of years. Rock grains by the billions have been washed down the mountainsides by rain-fed streams. Dried grains of rock have been scattered over the valley floor by shifting winds. In this picture, suggesting a seascape, a wind has formed the sand into wavelets, carried it up the gentle slopes of the dunes, and dropped it on their steeper far sides.

A valley glacier. This river of ice creeps slowly down Mt. Athabaska in the Canadian Rockies. Year after year it cuts its channel, grinding the rocks over which it moves. It carries along a great deal of sand and rock, which it piles up in ridges along its sides or at its foot. These ridges are called moraines. At the melting foot of this glacier begins the Athabaska River.

50

THE WORK OF ICE

Glaciers exist only where there is year-round snow. For they are themselves formed of snow which is piled up so very deep and heavy that it packs down under its own weight into a mass of ice. Then it can become a powerful force in erosion.

When a snowfield, high on a mountain slope, reaches a depth of about 100 feet, it begins to creep downward. Though a glacier is made of ice, which is a solid, it still has this ability to creep or flow. As it grows, from time to time it breaks loose from the mountain, tearing out great chunks of rock and leaving behind it an open space called a crevasse. This in time fills with snow again. As the process repeats, the glacier may eventually dig in the mountainside a large, curved hollow, called a cirque or amphitheater.

A glacier as it creeps acts like a plough, a sled, and a file, all at once. It ploughs up the soil of the valley, pushing it ahead and to either side. From ledges above, rock fragments shattered by frost tumble down the valley walls on to the glacier's broad back. Gradually these rocks settle down into the mass of the glacier. The glacier files and polishes, cuts and scrapes, by dragging its load of rocks across the valley floor. And the sides of the glacier grate against projecting crags and gradually wear them away too. So in the end all glaciated valleys are changed from V-shapes to U-shapes, with smooth, wide-apart walls.

These mountain-valley glaciers are small compared to the great ice sheets which have covered more than a quarter of the land on earth during the several great ice ages. These huge ice masses were thousands of feet thick and covered millions of square miles. They carved no jagged mountain scenes, as did the valley glaciers. Their enormous bulks crushed and scraped rugged areas like the highlands of Scotland and Ireland, the mountains of New York and New England, into rounded, gentler landscapes.

U-shaped valley. Smooth walls and a rounded floor are often found in once V-shaped valleys through which glaciers have passed. This is Crawford Notch, N. H. At left is the railroad; at right is the highway.

51

A glaciated landscape. Here, in the Canadian Rockies, the land has been broken by ice and frost to form rugged scenery. Glaciers grind rock off the valley walls. A long-vanished glacier scooped out the two small step lakes or tarns (centre and right) and filled them as it melted. Frost has crumbled the rocks. Lake Louise, seen at far left, is a glacier-made finger lake.

In addition to remodelling these highlands, the great ice sheets were important in the formation of thousands of lakes and rivers in North America, Europe, and northern Asia. They enlarged the Great Lakes and set the courses of great rivers such as the Ohio and the Missouri. As they melted, they dropped their loads of rocks, sand, and silt in great ridges called moraines and small, rounded hills called drumlins. Many of the hills in Wisconsin and Michigan, Martha's Vineyard and Nantucket, are moraines. Bunker Hill, outside Boston, is a drumlin. In some areas lakes formed when chunks of a glacier broke off, were covered with sand and rocks, melted, and left hollows which have since been kept filled by springs or streams.

LOOKING AHEAD

The age of the great ice sheets is not yet over. The ice caps on Greenland and Antarctica, with their 5 million cubic miles of ice, remind us of conditions faced by our human ancestors 10,000 years ago. But these ice caps—like all glaciers today—are gradually melting. If they melt entirely, the sea may some day—as often in the past—creep over many low-lying lands of the earth.

The Atlantic coastline of the United States from Massachusetts to Florida is sinking at the rate of 4 inches every hundred years. This may be the result not only of a rising sea level but of movements in the whole continental block.

The eastern United States is mostly what geologists call "old" countryside. Its mountains are rounded and worn down. Its valleys are broad and gentle, its rivers slow and winding. Its lowlands are carpeted with thick, rich soil.

In the western United States, too, the forces of erosion have been at work. But the earth's internal forces of uplift are far more active here than in the East. Many western states are strewn with lava, cinders, and ash from fairly recent volcanic eruptions. Lassen Peak in California is a dormant volcano which may erupt again at any time.

Most mountains of the West are high and young, with much bare rock and little soil. Their peaks stand towering and jagged, not yet shortened and rounded by wind and rain.

Also in the West, the crust of the earth seems uneasy. There is constant sideward slipping along the long San Andreas Fault in California. The state has many earthquakes.

The West has areas which are being pushed slowly, steadily upward. The Baldwin Hills area of the Los Angeles Plain has been arched upward at the rate of 3 feet in a hundred years. In the San Joaquin Valley to the north, the Buena Vista Hills are rising at the rate of 4 feet per century. This may not seem like much, but if it continues for 200,000 years, the Buena Vista Hills will be as high as the Cascade Mountains are today.

Meanwhile, in other parts of the earth's surface, changes are taking place too. The entire country of France appears to be tilting slowly northward, rising in the south, sinking along the Channel coast. If this movement continues, the waters of the Atlantic will one day cover great areas of northern France.

At the same time the Baltic Coast of Sweden is rising at the rate of ½ centimetre per year. If this rate of uplift is maintained for 10,000 years, all the water will be tilted out of the Baltic Sea.

So all around the world the uplift of mountains and plateaus is balanced by the slow downward warping of shorelines and inland basins, and by the destructive forces of rain, wind, frost, and ice. The only prediction that scientists can safely make now is that, as the ages pass, the earth's face will not remain the same. As a Greek philosopher said, 2,500 years ago, "There is nothing permanent in the world but change."

PART IV

THE CANOPY OF AIR

THE ATMOSPHERE, OUR HOME

MAN LIKES to think of himself as the conqueror of the world. Rarely would he compare himself to a fish. Yet man does live, fishlike, at the bottom of an ocean. This ocean is the atmosphere that blankets our planet.

Earth really is not one sphere but several fitted around one another. First is the lithosphere (sphere of stone), which is the earth's hard part. Nearly three fourths of it is covered by the hydrosphere (sphere of water), or oceans, averaging nearly 2 miles in depth. Around these spheres is wrapped the transparent, ever-moving atmosphere (sphere of air), hundreds of miles thick.

Only a small part of these spheres can support life. Plants and animals live mostly on or near the surface of the ground, in the upper levels of the sea, and in the lower levels of the atmosphere. This narrow band around the earth in which life can exist is called the biosphere.

Upon the atmosphere depends the world we know. Without it, the earth would be scorched by the sun on one side, frozen on the other. Deadly cosmic rays and showers of meteors would hammer the earth constantly. There would be no weather—no wind, rain, or clouds. There would be no erosion to weather rocks into soil. Sound would not exist, nor fire. There would be no plants, no animals, no life at all, without the atmosphere.

THE MAKE-UP OF AIR

The atmosphere is made up of many gases. At sea level, nitrogen forms 78 per cent of dry air; oxygen, 21 per cent; argon, 1 per cent; water vapour (made up of hydrogen and oxygen combined), 0.01 per cent to 4 per cent; carbon dioxide, about 0.03 per cent. There are also very small amounts of helium, xenon, and neon, and of some poisonous gases—ozone, methane, ammonia, carbon monoxide, and nitrous oxide.

The principal gases—oxygen, carbon dioxide, and nitrogen—are all necessary to life. Animals breathe in oxygen and breathe out carbon dioxide. Plants take in carbon dioxide and give off oxygen during the day; at night they take oxygen in.

The thin film of air that supports life on Earth is seen as a hazy layer, far below, in this picture taken from a U.S. Navy rocket 78 miles out in space. The heavens (at top) look black; for the blue sky, possible only where there is enough air to scatter sunlight, extends only about 12 miles out. Notice the slight curve of the horizon. Visible are parts of New Mexico, Colorado, Wyoming, Nebraska, South Dakota, and Utah. The diagonal green streak at left is the valley of the Rio Grande.

The use cycles of the gases in the atmosphere.

Both plants and animals need nitrogen in their diets. But nitrogen does not combine readily with other elements and cannot be taken by living things directly from the air.

The picture above shows how nitrogen is made usable. The trees and other plants in the bog (far left) contain nitrogen and carbon. As they decay, some of their carbon goes down into the soil. But the nitrogen and ammonia (ammonia is a compound of nitrogen and hydrogen) are released into the air as gases. Now, most plants and animals cannot use nitrogen in the form of gas, but certain bacteria can. These hold, or "fix," some of the nitrogen. They work in the soil and in the roots of clover and kindred plants. Animals eat the plants and get the nitrogen, which then goes through their systems and is dropped with their waste products. As these wastes decompose, nitrogen and some ammonia are returned to the air, to be used all over again. Some of the ammonia also goes into the soil, where it is turned into compounds called nitrites and nitrates, which are usable as plant food.

In the lake (upper left) the same sort of cycle is carried out. Nitrogen from the air is fixed by bacteria in the lake, or combines with some of the

hydrogen in the water to form ammonia. The ammonia is turned into nitrites and nitrates, which plants can use.

Near the centre of the picture, fuel containing carbon is being burned in a house; the fire uses oxygen and gives off carbon dioxide, as does the forest fire (background). Live trees absorb carbon dioxide and water from the soil, and give off oxygen. The cattle and horses inhale oxygen and exhale carbon dioxide, and their waste products contain methane. This gas combines with oxygen in the air to form more carbon dioxide.

Where does all this carbon dioxide go? Some is absorbed into the soil, and some by plants. The whole supply is renewed every 4 to 8 years (as compared to 3,000 years for oxygen, and 100 million years for nitrogen).

The sea is the earth's great reservoir of free carbon dioxide. It holds in solution 50 times the amount that hangs in the atmosphere. Some is carried into the sea by rain, some by streams bearing from the land carbonates and sediments rich in carbon dioxide.

In the sea, some carbon dioxide is absorbed by plants, which give off oxygen in turn. Some of the carbonates are used by sea animals to build their shells and bones. They breathe in oxygen and breathe out carbon dioxide. When they die and decay, still more carbon dioxide is given off, to be carried to the surface by currents of the sea.

Rainbows are caused by drops of water which break up sunlight into its different colors. Each drop acts as a tiny prism. A rainbow is seen in the sky directly opposite the observer. This is a double rainbow; note that the second has colours in reverse order. Some rainbows are triple; rarely, more are seen.

All over the world this interplay of earth, air, and living things maintains a delicate balance of use, release, and re-use for those elements of the air from which living things are largely made up—oxygen, water (hydrogen and oxygen), carbon, and nitrogen.

In outer space there are 1,000 particles of hydrogen and 100 particles of helium (the two lightest elements known) to every 10 to 20 particles of all other substances combined. But these two are relatively rare in our atmosphere. Scientists think that when our planet was forming, its force of gravity was not strong enough to prevent large quantities of these lightest elements from escaping into space.

The air as we know it was already created when the earth was still young. Volcanic gases from deep inside the earth came out as carbon dioxide, water vapour (which broke up into hydrogen and the first oxygen), and ammonia, which formed nitrogen compounds, since it contains nitrogen. Plant life, taking in carbon dioxide and giving off oxygen, probably produced most of the earth's present stock of free oxygen. And this stock made possible the rise of oxygen-breathing animals.

The atmosphere also incidentally contains pollen dust, bacteria, volcanic ash, salt particles from the sea, and "stardust" (meteoric material) from outer space, which falls to earth at the rate of 2,000 tons a day.

HIGH AS THE SKY

Air rapidly becomes less and less dense as you move out from the earth's surface. Six miles up, it is too thin to breathe. Twelve miles up, it no longer has enough oxygen to keep a candle burning. The greater the altitude, the fewer the molecules of any gas, and the greater the empty spaces between them. For every million molecules at sea level, there is only one 60 miles up.

The bottom layer of air, about 10 miles thick, is called the troposphere. It contains 75 percent of the atmosphere's weight. Around it, averaging 8 miles thick, lies the calm stratosphere. At about this level, a very important process takes place. Here the short-wave (ultra-violet) rays of the sunlight combine with oxygen to form a thin layer of a gas called ozone. Only a few of the ultra-violet rays get through this ozone layer and down to earth; they kill bacteria, prevent rickets, and cause sunburn. The long rays (infra-red) come through to give earth its warmth.

Above the stratosphere the chemosphere stretches out to about 50 miles from earth. Next, the ionosphere stretches from 50 to 250 miles up. And from 250 miles toward empty space extends the almost airless exosphere.

For 7 miles or so above the earth it gets steadily colder, because you are leaving the zone of solar heat reflected by the earth. The temperature drops to −81°F. at about 18 miles up. Then, in the ozone layer, the temperature rises again because so much sun's heat is being held there. About 50 miles out, the temperature drops once more, to −117°F., because the ozone has almost completely disappeared by then.

Beyond 50 miles man would not be able to feel the temperatures. For what we feel as heat is the

Auroras are beautiful, mysterious lights seen in the night sky most often in spring and fall. They appear to be caused by the sun. Jets of electrified particles from the sun speed toward the earth. Between 60 and 600 miles above the earth, the solar particles strike gas particles in our atmosphere and cause them to glow and vibrate. Auroras are seen most in the far north or far south, because the solar particles are turned toward the earth's poles as they enter the earth's magnetic field.

energy of molecules in motion, and the outer atmosphere has so few molecules that we would not respond to them. Nor is there enough air to protect us from either the fierce heat of the sun or the terrible cold of outer space. An unprotected person in space would be quickly broiled on the side facing the sun, frozen stiff on the other.

THE BRIGHT, BEAUTIFUL SKIES

Where does the colour in the sky come from? The sun's rays contain light of all the colours we know. Air molecules are just the right size to stop many of the blue rays and scatter them across the sky. We see the red and yellow of sunlight around us; the blue is in the sky.

This scattering of blue light occurs mainly in the lowest 12 miles of our atmosphere. Beyond that, the sky is violet. Beyond about 20 miles, there is only blackness.

Rainbows, halos, and coronas also result from the atmosphere's acting on sunlight. The light is bent or scattered by raindrops, tiny ice crystals, or droplets of cloud moisture. Different colours result.

A drapery aurora is one of the loveliest types. In some auroras, colours are even more spectacular. Different gases in our atmosphere give off light of different colours when struck by the solar radiation. Oxygen gives off green or red light; nitrogen, blue. In the northern hemisphere, auroras may be seen occasionally as far to the south as Florida and Mexico.

THE WANDERING WINDS

The sun's heat and the spinning of the earth cause our winds. Winds are possible because the atmosphere is made up of gases. The molecules of gases are free to move in all directions.

When warmed, air expands, lightens, and so rises. Cooler air moves in under it; and thus winds begin.

Now if the earth did not rotate, the air on the side of the earth facing the sun would keep being warmed. Getting lighter, it would rise and move straight to cooler areas. Air from cooler areas would move in under the departing warm air. All the earth's winds would move out from, and in toward, this area.

But the earth does rotate. At the equator the speed of rotation is about 1,000 miles per hour. As you go north or south, the speed decreases.

Because of this difference in speeds, air currents swirl as they pass over the earth's surface.

Warm air high above the earth is always moving outward from the tropics, and cold air is moving outward from the poles. Warm and cold air masses meet almost halfway between equator and poles. There they swing around the earth, high above it, in two great circles from west to east.

Most weather is probably related to the behaviour of these great circumpolar whirls. In summer the circumpolar whirl contracts, and warm air moves toward the pole. In winter the whirl edges two thirds of the way to the equator, carrying cold air over many lands.

How these great air movements are related to one another, and what they mean to us in terms of daily weather, is still only partly understood by our weather experts.

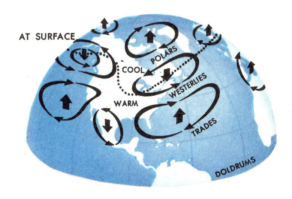

High-altitude winds. Arrows pointing from west to east show the north circumpolar whirl. Near the pole (arrows pointing down) are low-pressure cells. Near the equator are high-pressure cells (arrows pointing up) which carry the warm air north while others bring the icy polar air south.

Surface winds. Trade Winds come out of the northeast and travel east to west. Approaching land, they circle north. Westerlies bring cold air down from the poles over eastern United States, then circle north out to sea. Polar Easterlies swoop down from the pole in clockwise motion.

THE CHANGING WEATHER

The atmosphere is not a calm ocean of air, but a tossing sea laced with swift currents, furrowed by tremendous waves. And those currents and waves bring our weather.

Our daily weather comes to us in a procession of what meteorologists (weather experts) call high-pressure and low-pressure cells, or simply "highs" and "lows." A high is a large mass of cool,

relatively heavy air, usually several hundred miles wide, in which the movement of the winds is clockwise in the northern hemisphere, counterclockwise in the southern hemisphere. A low is a mass of warmer, relatively light air in which the winds move counterclockwise in the northern hemisphere, clockwise in the southern.

Highs and lows keep in fairly constant motion because of unequal heating of the earth by the sun and because of the earth's rotation. A high

Updrafts and downdrafts. Here we are looking south along the east slope of the Sierra Nevada. At right, beyond the picture, warm, moist air is rolling in from the Pacific Ocean. It is forced up and over the mountains. As it rises and cools, some of its moisture condenses and forms a cloud cap over the highest

peaks, 10,000 feet above the valley. On the east slope of the range, the air falls at the rate of 4,000 feet a minute and surges out over the valley, scooping up large quantities of dust. Five or 10 miles east, the air rises again. As it reaches the cooler upper levels, some of its moisture condenses and forms clouds.

forms where cooler air accumulates (as in the polar regions) and then follows a curving west-to-east path toward the equator, spreading outward as it goes. Lows form between highs that have different temperatures.

Local weather changes as highs and lows follow one another across the earth. The weather within a high is generally clear, dry, and sunny. But as the following low moves in, the warm air tends to rise and, as it cools, its water vapor may condense into rain.

Certain locations almost always have the same pressure condition—high or low. Near the equator is a zone of low pressure and warm, rising air known as the "doldrums." One of the three main zones of bad weather on earth is related to it; this zone is the Equatorial Convergence. There the Trade Winds from the northeast and the southeast come together, or converge. Both of these great wind systems carry masses of warm, moist air. Coming together, these masses soar upward. And in the cool heights rain begins.

The Equatorial Convergence rarely shifts more than 200 miles. But in the summer months, when the land areas are heated, it sometimes moves farther from the equator and may touch the two other great storm areas—the North and South Polar Fronts.

A "front" is the leading edge—usually very uneven—of any moving mass of warm or cold air. At the North and South Polar Fronts, cold air streaming out from the Polar Highs meets the warm air spreading northward and southward from the tropics. Cold air is heavier than warm air, so it creeps under the warm front, heading toward the equator. The warm front rides above it, cooling and forming clouds, mist, and rain.

Meteorologists speak of four kinds of fronts, which appear often on daily weather maps. These are cold, warm, occluded, and stationary fronts.

A cold front comes when a swift-moving cool air mass meets warm air and shoves it suddenly upward, often causing violent winds and thunderstorms, followed by clear skies.

A warm front develops when a warm air mass slowly slides over a cooler one. This slow action may cover a large area—perhaps several states. The warm air slowly cools and its vapour condenses into dreary rain, lasting perhaps days.

An occluded front develops when a cool front meets a warm front and hoists it completely off the ground, so that they meet high aloft—not at ground level. The weather then may have characteristics of both cold and warm storm fronts.

Once in a while a cold or warm front stands still. Until it moves on, it is called stationary.

A warm front. A mass of warm air (pink) is here riding up over a cool air mass. As it rises and cools, some of its moisture condenses into nimbo-stratus clouds—familiar rainmakers. Ahead (upper right) float high cirrus clouds, which often tell that a storm is on the way.

STORMS, LIGHTNING, AND RAIN

It is in zones of low pressure that storms begin. Storms come, as we know, in many forms, ranging from the light April shower to the blizzards of winter and the driving, heavy thunderstorms of summer. But the wildest of all storms is the hurricane, also called the typhoon. It is the terror not only of seamen but of landlubbers along the coasts, too.

How does a hurricane start? Somewhere in the doldrums, warmed moist air begins rising in a slow spiral over the ocean. More moist air moves in to replace it. As the air swirls up to cooler levels, its water vapour begins to condense into rain, releasing much heat in the process. Condensation releases more and more heat, the heated air swirls upward faster and faster, and the original slow spiral becomes a violent storm with winds circling at speeds up to 150 miles an hour. Across the ocean moves this hurricane, with an "eye" of calm air at its centre and death-dealing gales at its edges. For two weeks or so it threatens shipping and spreads destruction over any shores it touches. At last, its energies spent, it dies away.

Thunderstorms that form from the fleecy white cumulus clouds of sunny days are more familiar to us, but they form in much the same way as hurricanes. Thunderstorms have less moisture to work with and cannot travel as far or work up to such devastating proportions. Yet thunderstorms can be a majestic sight. Sometimes the cumulus clouds from which they form pile up to heights of 30,000 feet and more. They rise up until their tops bump against still higher air masses and flatten out.

A hurricane. A great mass of dense clouds whirls around the "eye," or area of calm. The top of the clear eye can be seen in the upper left corner. As in all low-pressure areas, the winds always whirl counterclockwise in the northern hemisphere, clockwise in the southern.

Inside these thunderheads, droplets of water are continually swept about by violent updrafts and downdrafts. They may freeze into hail, or evaporate into invisible vapour, or fall as rain.

But how does rain form?

In the very high clouds, it is believed, water vapour gathers around tiny crystals of ice until they are heavy enough to fall. On reaching warmer levels, they melt and fall as rain. In lower clouds each water droplet forms probably about some tiny particle of dust or salt floating in the air.

Electricity, too, seems to have an important part in rain. Each water droplet has an electrical charge. But each droplet is surrounded by air molecules carrying an opposite charge which neutralises the droplet's charge. It is believed that a cloud can shed rain only when something happens to upset this balance.

Perhaps a sudden updraft sweeps the air molecules to the upper part of the cloud. Then the charged droplets can gather, grow heavy, and fall, gathering others as they go. And down comes the rain.

Congested cumulus clouds. Piling up over warm land on a humid day, these clouds may drop showers. They are a type of cloud midway between the fair-weather clouds at left and the thunderheads that appear below.

What is a thunderstorm? How does a lightning flash happen?

At times the negative charge within a cloud builds up tremendously. When the "negative potential" rises to between 10 million and 100 million volts, then it must be relieved. An electrical discharge either within the cloud or from the cloud to earth is necessary to accomplish this, for earth has a positive charge.

The swift flashes of electricity travelling between earth and cloud charge and electrically excite molecules of air all along the path. These heated molecules glow, and it is their glow that we see as a flash of lightning.

The air suddenly expands as it is heated, and this expansion sets up vibrations—sharp, sudden movements—in the air. When these vibrations reach our ears, we call them thunder.

Distant thunderheads forming from summer cumulus clouds take the shape of giant anvils as their tops are levelled by relatively stable air layers miles high.

A thunderstorm. At times the negative electricity in part of a cloud builds up far beyond the positive charge. When the negative potential reaches 10 to 100 million volts, there is a quick discharge within the cloud, or between the cloud and the earth, which has a positive charge. The electricity shooting through the air causes gases in it to glow as lightning. In suddenly heating the air in its path, the electrical discharge also causes it to expand violently. This expansion starts the vibrations of air which we call thunder. Beyond the thunderstorm in this Arizona desert scene is a procession of fair-weather cumulus clouds which may, in their turn, thicken and produce a thunderstorm. Notice, incidentally, the typical flat bottoms of these cumulus clouds. In the various shapes of clouds the directions and force of air currents are revealed.

WATER VAPOUR AND CLOUDS

If all the moisture in the atmosphere suddenly fell at once, it would cover the earth with a layer of water only one inch deep. Yet water vapour— water in evaporated form—is one of the most important gases in the air. It holds much of the heat being radiated from the earth's surface. Moving with the winds, water vapour also helps to make cool places warmer, and vice versa.

Without moisture in our atmosphere, suffocating dust clouds would roll over the earth. The temperature would rise and fall to dreadful extremes. In fact, without moisture there would be neither weather nor life on earth.

On clear, dry days the moisture is invisible vapour. We see the moisture when it falls as rain, hail, or snow; when it appears on the grass as dew or frost; when it coats trees with ice. We see it when tiny droplets (5 billion to a teaspoon!) shroud the earth in fog or ride the air as clouds.

Whether moisture will be visible depends mainly on temperature. Warm **air can hold more moisture in the invisible, transparent form of vapour than** cool air. When moist air is cooled, condensation takes place. Some of the **vapour turns to liquid droplets which can be seen.**

Sometimes after sundown, when the earth gives up the sun's heat, the lower air cools. Fog forms in the hollows, or drops of dew form on the cool ground.

Sometimes winds carry warm moist air over cool surfaces, forming fog or low banks of stratus clouds (page 64). Moist breezes from the sea blowing in over winter-frozen land produce wet fogs. Or warm summer air may blow out from land over the cooler sea and form a sea fog.

Moist warm air simply brushing against a cold glass will deposit some of its water as drops on the outside of the glass.

Warm air may be cooled by rising as well as by travelling over a cool surface. When it reaches cool enough heights, clouds form. On sunny days these are often cumulus clouds (pages 66-67). Each cloud is really the top of a column of air, invisible until its water vapor condenses into a cloud.

Warm air pushed up a mountainside will also cool; so many mountains wear caps of cloud.

CLIMATE AND HISTORY

Weather changes from day to day. Climates change over long periods. Today our climates are growing slowly warmer. The rivers of ice in high mountains, the ice caps over the poles, are melting. We are living toward the end of a million-year-long Ice Age.

This Ice Age has included all the history of man. Man has never known the mild, normal climate of this planet. For most of the earth's history, the polar regions were free of ice. Temperatures were mild all over the earth. Animals ranged more widely, and plants spread over the areas that are barren today.

Much more recently, changes in climate have influenced human history. Long wet and dry periods have produced jungles or deserts where civilizations once flourished. Many pueblos of the American Southwest were abandoned when land around them became too dry for farming. On the contrary, cities of the Mayan and Cambodian peoples, in Mexico and Indo-China, were swallowed up by jungles during centuries of heavy rainfall, and these had to be abandoned too.

The best climate for high civilization may be one with stimulating, changeable weather, moderate temperatures, and sufficient rainfall. Historians tell us that rainfall was declining when both the Greek and Roman civilizations declined. **More favourable climate is enjoyed today by much** of northern Europe, Great Britain, and parts of the Soviet Union, as well as the United States.

But will we always have the climate we have today? Our land is warming up, perhaps because we have so many factories, pouring out 6 billion tons of carbon dioxide each year; and we have fewer forests to use up the carbon dioxide and give off oxygen to keep the balance.

The carbon dioxide in the atmosphere has increased by 10 percent in the last 50 years. It tends to make the earth warmer because, being a heavy gas, it helps to prevent radiation of heat from the earth's surface. Man himself, then, may be a cause of our warming climate.

Cirrus clouds are the highest of the familiar types. They often ride 8 miles or more above the earth, and often tell of bad weather to come. The clouds here are seen at sunset.

THE PAGEANT OF LIFE

WHEN LIFE BEGAN

FOR MUCH of the long span of its history, our planet lay barren and lifeless. The waters of its oceans rose and fell in tides and stirred under the winds. But in them nothing living moved. Above them the continents loomed, bleak as the landscapes of the moon.

Perhaps as much as 2½ billion years ago, life mysteriously appeared in the waters. Scientists do not yet know how. But this is sure: there came into being very tiny bits of matter that could be called "living." They may have been created by the action of sunlight upon chemicals in the warm ancient seas. Perhaps they were like the viruses which scientists study today—very complicated chains of atoms that form molecules, which in some ways seem to have the nature of living things and in other ways seem lifeless. Whatever actually happened, we do know that from such shadowy beginnings have come all the wondrous living things we know—the hordes of flying, swimming, crawling, and walking creatures; the countless shrubs and trees, grasses and mosses, ferns and flowers, which brighten our world.

Man has told countless stories of the creation of life, but not until around the year 1800 did he begin reading the true story as told by fossils in the rocks of the earth's crust. Fossils are the remains or traces of living things of the past—skeletons or imprints, for example—found in rock. Probably you have seen in polished stone the pattern of a leaf, or the outline of a snail. That leaf or snail lived and died perhaps millions of years ago. It became buried in mud or sand. Layer on layer, the covering piled up until pressure and chemical action changed the soil into rock. The frail leaf mouldered away, but its shape was preserved in the rock. The snail shell was preserved, too, distinct from the rock around it. So in the rock today we still see the shape of the fossil leaf or the actual shell of the snail.

Fossils have been found of many plants and animals no man has ever seen alive. But the book of the rocks tells us that they lived and something of what they looked like. Through figuring the age of the rocks, we can tell about when these things lived. Scientists who study fossils are called palaeontologists, and their science is palaeontology—the science of ancient life. Their work leads us back more than 1,000 million years to the very dawn of life.

A trilobite fossil. In the primeval sea, 500 million years ago, lived hard-shelled, many-legged creatures we call trilobites. No one living today has ever seen one. But we find their outlines in rock—fossils like this. Sediments falling on the sea bottom covered the trilobite after it died; as the sediment hardened into rock and replaced the decayed animal, this shape was preserved. Few trilobites were more than 12 inches long, but they dominated their age.

THE MORNING OF LIFE

The study of changes in the earth's crust through the ages, and of ancient life as revealed by fossils, is like working a giant jigsaw puzzle. The scientist studies the earth's crust for its traces of mountain building, volcanic action, erosion, flooding, laying down of sediments that form rock layers, and all the other forces that keep changing the earth's surface. He uses the best available knowledge of animals and plants. Finally, he puts all the puzzle pieces together. Some parts of the picture are not clear; some pieces do not fit together properly; some are missing. But year by year the picture does grow more complete.

This history seems to fall into several great divisions. For millions of years the earth's surface and its climates change slowly, and changes in plant and animal life are likewise slow. Then comes a time of catastrophic change—mountain building, flooding of the land by seas, or warming or cooling of the climate. Then animal and plant types change suddenly.

The chart on this page shows how science has divided the first 2 billion years of life into three great eras, each divided into shorter periods.

The number of years for each period is only an estimate—a good guess. But each period did follow great changes in the earth's surface, and important changes in forms of life occurred.

In the chart we see how life began with the nameless soft-bodied creatures of which little trace remains. Then came the crablike trilobites, the nautiloids and other shellfish, and the sea scorpions, which were among the first creatures to venture out of the sea. The fishes began the great line of vertebrates, or backboned animals. Amphibians were the first vertebrates to spread across the land; then the reptiles became dominant, and finally the mammals (charted on pages 86-87).

But now let us go back and read the story.

During its first billion—perhaps two billion—years, the earth was barren. Mountains rose and crumbled, seas advanced and retreated, and these changes left their marks in the oldest rocks. But of life then we find no clear evidence.

The first creatures whose fossils are found in large numbers date from the period called the Cambrian, which dawned 500 million years ago. For perhaps 500 million years before that, there had been life on earth, but these earlier, simpler, soft-bodied animals left no enduring remains.

The first living beings were perhaps too small for even a microscope to show. Gradually they developed into very simple, one-celled animals of the kind we call protozoa. The protozoa developed most of the basic mechanics of living—digesting food, moving about, and reproducing themselves from two parent cells. The fact of two parents, rather than one, was very important, because this made possible different combinations of traits and gradual changes in life forms.

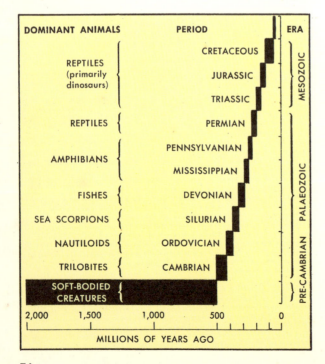

DOMINANT ANIMALS	PERIOD	ERA
REPTILES (primarily dinosaurs)	CRETACEOUS	MESOZOIC
	JURASSIC	
	TRIASSIC	
REPTILES	PERMIAN	PALAEOZOIC
AMPHIBIANS	PENNSYLVANIAN	
	MISSISSIPPIAN	
FISHES	DEVONIAN	
SEA SCORPIONS	SILURIAN	
NAUTILOIDS	ORDOVICIAN	
TRILOBITES	CAMBRIAN	
SOFT-BODIED CREATURES		PRE-CAMBRIAN

MILLIONS OF YEARS AGO
2,000   1,500   1,000   500   0

Life through the ages. Across the bottom of this chart you can count the number of years it covers. At far right are names of the grand eras of life; also, names of periods. Palaeozoic means the era of ancient life; Mesozoic, the era of "middle life." Periods are named after regions where rock layers typical of the periods occur; for example, "Cambrian" from Cambria, the Latin name of Wales, and "Devonian" from Devon, England. At left are listed animals dominant in each period. On pages 86-87 is a chart for the Cenozoic ("recent" life) era. Pre-Cambrian, Palaeozoic, and Mesozoic covered perhaps 2,000 million years. The Cenozoic Era, in which we live, is only 75 million years old.

The age of trilobites. The giant in the centre is a trilobite perhaps a foot long. Smaller ones are behind him. Most of these life forms of the Cambrian sea bottoms look like plants but are really colonies of animals. Reddish sponges are seen at left and in the background. The balloon shapes (centre foreground) are glass sponges. At top left floats an almost transparent jellyfish; at top right, an early shrimplike arthropod. At bottom toward left, in front of the worm, is an early snail; to its right are two-shelled brachiopods—extinct shellfish types.

Probably these developments from the first live molecules to the many colourful tiny protozoa took many hundreds of millions of years—as much time as all that has passed since!

The next stage was probably the joining of groups of protozoa in sticky masses like *Volvox*. From these colonies developed many-celled animals. Henceforth more and more complicated and specialised living things developed, while the simple, one-celled animals and plants went on.

Jellyfish and polyps were first to develop mouths and stomachs. Flatworms had the first nervous systems and "brains." By the beginning of the Cambrian period, nervous systems, digestive tracts, and sensory organs (eyes, mouths, feelers, etc.) had all appeared in sea animals.

During the Cambrian, the big development was hard parts: protective shells, plates, and skins—parts that could leave fossil traces. Snails and other mollusks developed, including types still numerous today. Sponges—whole colonies of simple animals with a tough framework—spread across the sea floors. Many other types appeared, flourished for 100 million years or more, then faded away.

The most successful animals of the Cambrian were the arthropods. Nowadays, the arthropods we know best are the insects; but in Cambrian times shrimplike arthropods dominated. Most successful of all were the crablike trilobites.

After 80 million years the seas rose up in perhaps the greatest flood of all time. A new age began—the Ordovician, with a mild climate and vast oceans. Sea animals grew larger, more varied. More of them had shells. Corals piled up their skeleton cities. The first clams appeared—and starfish that feasted on them. Dominant now were the mollusks called nautiloids, in shell cases up to 15 feet long.

The Ordovician slid quietly into the 40 million years of the Silurian. The trilobites were fewer, but shellfish of all kinds multiplied. The largest new creatures were the sea scorpions—some of them 9 feet long.

In the Silurian the first true fishes appeared. Up to now, living things had been invertebrates—that is, without backbones, but usually with their hard parts on the outside, as spines or shells. When the first fishes appeared with a framework of bones inside, the Age of Vertebrates dawned. It is still going on. Almost all the animals we know above insect size are vertebrates. So are we.

The age of nautiloids. The giant here is a nautiloid—a 15-foot mollusk of the type called cephalopods ("head-footed ones") because their tentacles, or "feet," grew out of their heads. Cephalopods ruled the seas of this period—the Ordovician. They were meat eaters and probably ate trilobites. At bottom, from left, are trilobites, snail, clams, pink graptolite (a cluster of tiny shelled animals), two-shelled brachiopods, some

The age of sea scorpions. Across the upper left in this Silurian scene hurry two long-armed sea scorpions. In the centre of the picture lies another one—a 9-foot giant. The tall, waving "flowers" in the scene are Silurian crinoids; note how they differ from the Ordovician crinoids in the upper picture on this page. In the extreme upper left corner are a pair of swimming pink shellfish called ostracods. At lower left is a

starfish (near the giant snail), another snail (facing us), two horn corals (like strange potted plants), and at the right a tall crinoid, or sea lily—a flowerlike animal with a long stem and arms like flower petals. The low mass next to it is coral. At top right swims an early sea scorpion, above a graptolite community. (Compare this sea scorpion with the giants in the picture below.) At upper right are small trilobites and nautiloids.

coiled nautiloid, related to the straight-shelled giant of the Ordovician (upper picture). Beneath the nautiloid are a trilobite and sea worms; to their right are sponges, corals, and the mosslike animals called bryozoans. Under the giant sea scorpion's claws are a fishlike anaspid and a king crab. At far right are a group of possible ancestors of modern fishes. The first true jawed fish (extreme right) is 2 to 3 inches long.

A Devonian shoreline. In the water, left, are thick seaweeds, **Nematophyton,** perhaps among the first plants to move ashore. Their tubed trunks brought them water. The tall, fuzzy-stemmed plant at left is **Psilophyton,** typical of many early land plants, including the almost tree-size plants at left centre **(Duisbergia)** and right centre **(Pseudosporochnus).** These have simple leaves growing from stems to catch sunlight. At bottom left are a scorpion and a millipede, two of the first land-dwelling animals. In the pool at right lungfishes frolic, and in the lower right corner crawls little **Ichthyostega,** the world's first amphibian.

LIFE SPREADS TO THE LAND

Late in the Silurian period, the earth's crust buckled. New mountains rose, much land was lifted up, and the waters flowed back into the ocean basins. And life began to spread from the shrinking seas to marshes and newly dry land.

For perhaps a billion years, sea plants had changed little. Now some were living outside the water; they spread a film of green over rocks and over the rich layers of sediment left by the retreating seas.

Then, astonishingly, in a space of 50 billion years—relatively a short time—plants appeared in countless new forms, such as ferns and great cone-bearing trees and leafy plants. At first they stayed along marshy shores. Before they could survive on higher, dry land, they had to develop roots to go down into the soil for water, and branches to thrust upward and scatter spores through the air.

The first land plants had only leafless stems containing tubes to bring up water. Tiny hairs attached the stems to the soil. Later plants had branches which reached down for water and became roots. Then came plants with simple leaves to catch sunlight needed for growth. Finally appeared plants with true leaves.

Early plants did not cast off seeds that would

grow into plants just like themselves. They threw off, instead, tiny spores. The spores grew into flat sheets called gametophytes. These tiny, heart-shaped gametophytes, clinging to the damp earth, produced sperm (male) cells and egg (female) cells. These cells would combine to start new plants, but they could do so only in water. This process meant that plants had to stay close to water if they were to produce new plants.

Later, plants developed true seeds. The male sperm from these plants could be carried in wind-blown pollen to the female egg cells. When they joined, new plants grew.

With this new method of reproduction, plants could multiply on dry land. Gradually the barren rocks of the earth became covered with green. Now there was food on land as well as among the algae and other seaweeds. So animals, too, could live on the land.

The first animals to thrive ashore were arthropods. These were ancestors of the more than 800,000 kinds of insect species of today. In those days the arthropods were mostly spiders, scorpions, and millipedes.

Next, fish began to appear with body parts for breathing oxygen directly from air instead of from water. During dry spells they could live on mud flats after the water disappeared. Lungfish could lie still in the mud and breathe; other types developed strong fins, with which they could drag themselves along. From these fins developed the feet of the first amphibian.

Fins to feet! Transforming a fish into an amphibian sounds like magic. But the gradual changes—over millions and millions of years—by which this happened are no more remarkable than the rest of life's history. Life forms are ever changing, ever new.

The age of reptiles. On these two pages is a panorama of animals that lived in the first part of the Mesozoic Era, from the Coal Age (left) through the Permian (middle) to the Jurassic (right). At far left, drinking from this pond of the Coal Age, is **Eryops**, a mostly land-dwelling amphibian. Little **Seymouria**, on the island, may have been the first true reptile. The next three reptiles (two on bank of pond, one crossing log) were Permian fish-eaters. The next two (fins on backs) were meat-eaters; the third finback was a plant-

REPTILES TAKE OVER THE EARTH

As the Devonian period drew to a close, among its marshes and ponds appeared the first amphibians. Like all amphibians, including our frog, they laid eggs in the water. The eggs hatched into larvae or tadpoles. After these grew to adulthood, they lived on the land.

The early amphibians multiplied rapidly in the Mississippian and Pennsylvanian (Coal Age) periods. For 50 million years climates were mild, and the earth was green with marshlands from Greenland to Antarctica. Ferns, rushes, and other

plants grew thickly, died, and piled up in huge rotting layers which became our beds of coal. Insect life flourished in this warm, damp world, which saw such monsters as the 29-inch dragonfly. But the short-legged, heavy-bodied, slow amphibians prospered most. Some grew to a length of 10 to 15 feet. Most developed an increasing ability to live on land.

Great new changes brought in the Permian period. Huge mountain ranges, the Appalachians and the Urals, were thrust up. Inland waters receded, swamps dried, glaciers crept across the land. The soft trees of swamps gave way to cone-

eater, hunted by the others. In the Triassic, many reptiles walked increasingly on their hind legs, while their forelegs became short arms suitable for grasping. The small, stripe-backed **Saltoposuchus** running along in the foreground is believed to have been the ancestor of fearsome dinosaurs to come in the Jurassic and Cretaceous. **Plateosaurus**, looming behind him, was the first of the giants. Tiny **Podokesaurus** (right) was an early meat-eating dinosaur. **Cynognathus** (lower right) was an ancestor of mammals.

bearers (ancestors of our pines and firs) and cycads (intermediate between palms and firs). It was a new, less friendly world for land animals.

A few amphibians went back to the water. Others lived entirely on land, and their young grew up without a tadpole stage. They became the reptiles that ruled the next age of life and led the way to higher forms.

Wandering over dry land, reptiles ate meat instead of fish, land plants instead of seaweeds. The climate warmed up again, and reptiles multiplied. During the 30 million years of the Triassic period and the 25 million of the Jurassic, reptiles de-

veloped many differing families. Turtles reached almost their present forms; snakes and lizards likewise. Some reptiles developed winglike limbs and flew, such as the leather-winged and feather-less pterosaurs, and the later pteranodons, with a wingspread of 27 feet. Toothy, wingless waterfowl swam the seas. But it was a member of another branch, *Archaeopteryx*, which in the Jurassic appeared as the first true bird.

Some reptiles, meanwhile, returned to the sea. Among the early sea reptiles were the ichthyosaurs, more than 25 feet long, with small, finlike limbs and forked, fishy tails. They seemed well

The rule of the dinosaurs. The picture on these two pages continues the panorama of reptiles from the Jurassic period (left) through the Cretaceous (right). At left, bottom, we see swift, red, tiny **Compsognathus**, probably an egg-stealing hunter and perhaps an ancestor of giant carnivores to come. The bluish reptile just beyond him is stupid, plant-eating **Camptosaurus**, fine prey for the huge, 30-foot-long **Allosaurus** to his right, tyrant of the Jurassic period. Perhaps the only creature **Allosaurus** could not frighten was the first

suited to water living, yet were the first of the reptile giants to vanish as the age of reptiles ended.

The main line of reptiles grew from a small, swift, lively sort that ran on their hind legs. Their forelegs became arms; their legs were muscular; their jaws held sharp, needle-like teeth. These small four-footed creatures, called *Saltoposuchus*, were the ancestors of modern birds—and of the largest, most fearsome land animals of all time—the "terrible lizards," or dinosaurs.

THE AGE OF DINOSAURS

For almost 100 million years, the dinosaurs ruled the earth. Ranging the moist, warming plains of the continents, some grew to enormous sizes. Some still ate plants, but others killed and ate animals. Some strode on two legs, others on four.

An early giant was the plant-eating *Plateosaurus*, as much as 20 feet from head to tip of tail. Early meat-eaters included two tiny, swift robbers, *Podekesaurus* and *Compsognathus*,

bird, **Archaeopteryx,** flying in centre foreground. As the seas rose in the Cretaceous period, huge dinosaurs flourished. One was **Brontosaurus** (extreme right), which stayed in shallow water to take the weight off his feet. A leathery, featherless flying reptile, **Rhamphorynchus,** is flying over **Brontosaurus.** Along the shore (background) waddles **Stegosaurus,** weighted down by his probably useless spine plates. Plants of this warm period resemble ferns more than they do the cone-bearing trees of colder times (pages 80-81).

which probably made off with the eggs of their big, clumsy relatives. As time rolled on, there were huge meat-eaters too. Terror of the late Jurassic plains and forests was *Allosaurus*, a 30-foot monster with rows of knifelike teeth and savage claws to hold its prey. Perhaps the only creature safe from this frightful beast was *Archaeopteryx*, the first bird.

But the greatest age of dinosaurs lay ahead. During the late Jurassic and the Cretaceous, the warm seas rose again, flooding over much of

Europe and almost half of North America. Palm trees grew in Alaska, and figs and breadfruit in Greenland. Corals built their reefs as far north as Canada. And the warm climate favoured the dinosaurs more than ever, because like all reptiles they need warmth to be really active.

Over the warm, low-lying lands and through the vast stretches of swampland waddled the great plant-eating dinosaurs, growing fat on the thick vegetation. They grew larger and larger. And their principal enemies, the meat-eating

dinosaurs, lived in such luxury as they had never before known.

The great plant-eating monsters, with vast swamps to feed on, grew into the hugest animals that ever trod the earth. Greatest of these swamp giants was *Brontosaurus* ("thunder lizard"), 30 tons and 70 feet from the tip of his tail to his small head, with its broad, dull teeth and little brain. To support his enormous weight, he had four pillar-like legs—and even then he stayed mostly in shallow waters which would buoy him up.

Stegosaurus, belonging to another order of dinosaurs, was just as amazing—low-slung, hump-backed, with strange, heavy, triangular plates standing up from its 20-foot spine from tiny pointed head to tail. *Stegosaurus* and *Brontosaurus* each had an extra nerve centre in the spine

to control the hind legs. These "extra brains" were larger than their tiny real brains. *Stegosaurus'* real brain weighed only about 2½ ounces—as much as a small dog's—and his spinal centre weighed 20 times as much.

Some later dinosaurs lived in the uplands, often on open plains. For protection against enemies many had such special equipment as thick, spiked **armoured plates** and a tail like a club of bone, or horns as sharp as spears and a thick helmet of bone over a 7-foot skull. One had a flat "duck" bill for cropping water plants and a mouth almost solidly paved with 2,000 teeth to grind these plants to a pulp.

But 2,000 flat teeth were little protection against the Cretaceous *Tyrannosaurus rex,* king of all the dinosaurs. The mightiest and most fear-

King of the tyrants. Dinosaurs protected themselves in various ways. Some wore armour, spiked and studded, like **Ankylosaurus** in left foreground. Some wore frilled bone helmets, like **Triceratops** at right, and fought with three sharp horns. At far right, background, is **Struthiomimus,** which like the ostrich depended on long legs and speed. Heading for the water at left is flat-skulled, duck-billed **Anatosaurus.** They all needed protection against gigantic **Tyrannosaurus rex,** king of the tyrants, the bloodthirsty monster that dominates the Cretaceous scene here. Only the enormous flying reptile in the distance, **Pteranodon,** appears safe.

Flowering plants became dominant in the Cretaceous period. This development was more important than any development in the animal world then. Magnolias (right foreground), dogwood, and laurel (behind **Tyrannosaurus**) blossomed along with sassafras. There were groves of oaks (behind dogwood), willows (upper right), as well as fan palms and palmettos (centre foreground). Aided by bees and insects, the flowering plants prospered down to our time.

some flesh-eater ever known, from nose to tail he measured 50 feet, with his terrible head 18 to 20 feet above the ground. His rows of 6-inch teeth were as sharp as sabres.

Tyrannosaurus feared no creature, yet at the end of the Cretaceous his kind vanished along with the other dinosaurs.

What happened? Were the hot summers and the colder winters too much for these sluggish beasts? Did the small mammals which were developing across the lands eat the unguarded dinosaur eggs? Did changes in plant life leave the big reptiles without enough food?

Such reasons could account for the disappearance of land reptiles, but not for the doom of those in the sea. Largest of these was *Plesiosaur,* up to 50 feet in length. Some had long, thin necks

and short heads, others long heads and short necks. Instead of legs they had flippers like a turtle's, with which they swam slowly through the waters. Slowness was no handicap, for their heads could swing almost 40 feet from side to side, to snap at passing fish, and their teeth were long and sharp. And there were also huge lizards in the sea, ranging up to 25 feet in length. These *Mosasaurs* were the fiercest pirates of all, but at the end of the Cretaceous they vanished with the rest. Of all the reptiles that once tramped the land, swam the seas, and glided through the air, only turtles, crocodiles, snakes, and lizards remain.

Whatever caused it, the decline of the reptiles at the end of the Cretaceous, 75 million years ago, opened the way for a new class of animals—the mammals, to which we ourselves belong.

WOOLLY MAMMOTH

GIGANTOCAMELUS

AMEBELODON

MEGACAMELUS

MIOCENE

SYNDYOCERAS

PROCAMELUS

BRONTOPS

30 MILLION
YEARS AGO

POËBROTHERIUM

OLIGOCENE

40 MILLION
YEARS AGO

UINTATHERIUM

EOCENE

PROTYLOPUS

60 MILLION
YEARS AGO

BARYLAMBDA

PALEOCENE

TETRACLAENODON

75 MILLION
YEARS AGO

Six periods of the Cenozoic. The Cretaceous period—the last in the Mesozoic Era, or Age of Reptiles—
ended with widespread movements of the earth's crust, changes in sea level, and a cooler climate. Just
when the reptiles seemed to have completely established themselves as leaders in the pageant of life,
they suddenly had to face new living conditions—and failed. Life went on, but now with a very differently
patterned, differently behaving group of animals in the lead—the mammals. As a mammal himself, man
likes to think that Nature had experimented enough with great size and weight, with fearsome teeth and
claws, with all the ponderous armour which dinosaurs carried for defence. It is a fact that the animals
which now rose to power were creatures that depended more on speed, agility, warm-bloodness, and—
most important of all—intelligence. The earliest of these creatures—furtive little animals like shrews and
moles—had appeared as far back as the Jurassic. At the close of the Cretaceous, when new ways of
survival were demanded, it was these scurrying little early mammals—not the thunder-footed reptiles—

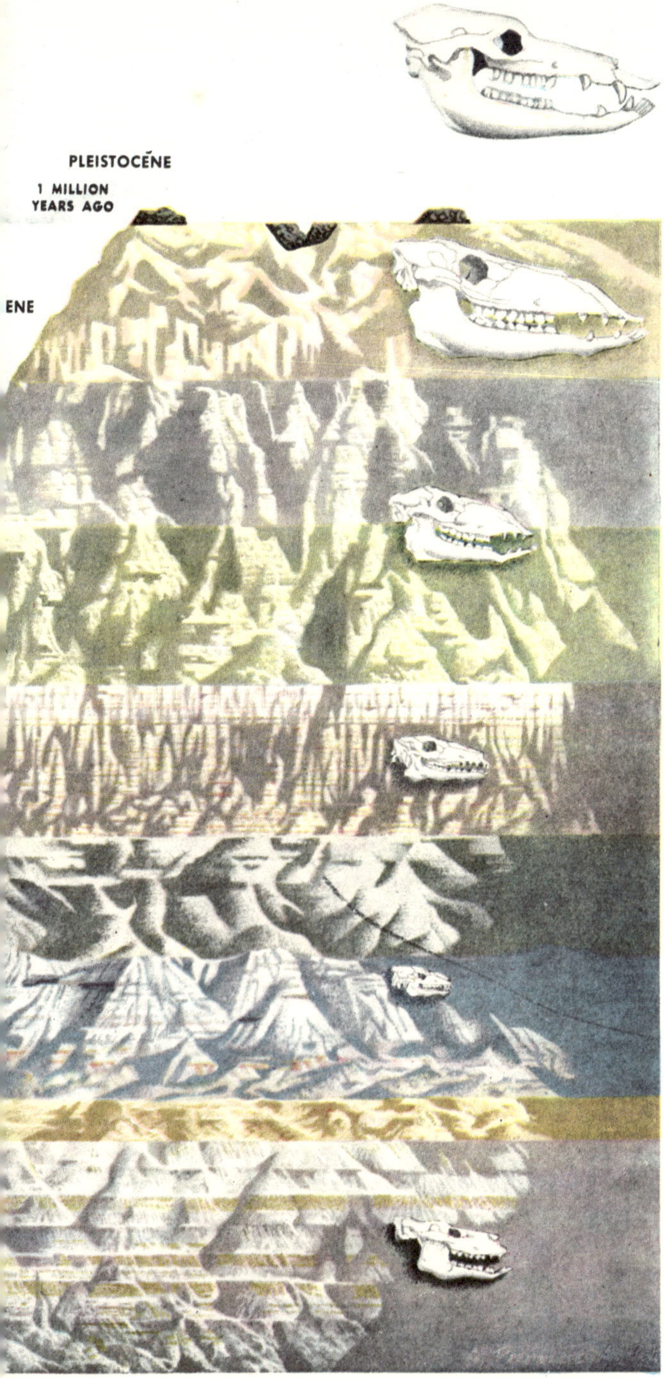

PART VI

THE AGE OF MAMMALS

PLEISTOCÉNE
1 MILLION
YEARS AGO

ENE

that endured. Not all the mammals, by any means, multiplied and fathered new, more successful forms. But the basic plan of their life—body temperature control, care of the young, and stress on intelligence—was a success. From the start of the Cenozoic ("recent life") Era, mammals branched out into the diversified forms seen here, and into many others also—including man. Rock layers, from Paleocene (earliest) to Pleistocene, represent all Cenozoic periods except our own, called Recent. At left, opposite the rock layers, are animals characteristic of each of the periods.

WHY MAMMALS?

WHEN THE first mammals appeared, dinosaurs were still the rulers of the earth. Surrounded by huge, hungry, thunder-footed giants, many of the timid mammals—not much larger than rats and mice today—may have stayed in the shadows of the swamps or in the high branches of the soft-wood trees.

To have seen them at any time in that first million years of their existence, no one would have thought that mammals would one day rule the earth, as they do now. How has it come about?

Mammals have several advantages over the earlier vertebrates. For one thing, they are warm-blooded; that is, they have built-in automatic temperature controls which keep their bodies at about the same temperature in either cold or warm weather. Most of them have furry coats to hold in their body heat in winter, and other ways to get rid of body heat in summer. The dinosaurs, lacking such body equipment, became so cold and sluggish in cold weather that they could not hunt food, defend themselves against enemies, or move to warmer areas.

Mammals have other advantages, too. Instead of laying eggs they bear their young alive. They do not run the risk—which the dinosaurs ran—of having their eggs eaten by others. Also, mammals care for their young. A mammal mother feeds her babies milk which she prepares in her body, and she teaches them.

Mammals can learn more than other animals. They have larger brains, greater curiosity. The more the young mammal learns from his parents,

The Eocene in North-America. Among armadillos, anteaters, and sloths, monkey-like creatures (lower left) appeared which were the first animals to have close-set, depth-perceiving eyes like man's. They ranged both Americas, but died out in North America during the Eocene, making way for rodents developing from such types as little squirrel-like forms to the right of the monkey-like creatures here. There were early horses—

the more likely he is to grow up and have young of his own. Mammals of long ago thus tended to survive in larger numbers and pass their traits on to new generations.

Most important for mammals was the gradual improvement of their brains. More and more, they used intelligence, rather than size and strength, to deal with the environment. More and more, individuals survived life's dangers because, having better brains, they could change their behavior to meet new conditions.

DAWN OF THE MAMMALS' DAY

At the dawn of the Paleocene period, the dinosaurs were gone. Of the whole vast reptile family, only a few alligators, turtles, snakes, and lizards remained. Now that it was safer to live on the ground, the small mammals—many of which had previously spent most of their time in the trees—were free to develop new ways of life below.

In America, the shallow inland sea withdrew, and the Rockies rose up. The climate was still

Eohippus (Hyracotherium), at lower left, and horselike cousins, **Paleosyops**, just above. There were catlike hunters, and packs of doglike ones, as **Mesonyx** snarling in the foreground; and there was weasel-like **Tritemnedon** (above, to left of bird **Diatryma**). Awkward, many-horned giants at right (front and rear) are **Uintatherium** and **Eobasileus**. **Hyrachyus**, ancestor of a group of rhinos, is in the extreme right corner.

gentle. Tropical plants—figs, breadfruits, palmettos—bloomed across the moist lowlands as the mammals diversified and spread across the hospitable land. Once more earth teemed with life.

The new way of living brought many changes to early mammals. Those that came down from the trees had less need for claws, so handy for climbing. Claws began to disappear in some types, and hoofs—better for running—replaced them. Some animals gave up their diet of plants or insects and experimented with hunting and with eating meat. Important in the Paleocene were ancestors of the shrews, a marsupial ancestor of the opossum, and small, horse-headed, cat-bodied ancestors of today's hoofed animals.

The Eocene's monkey-like creatures with close-set, depth-perceiving eyes were perhaps man's earliest cousins. Other mammals included the awkward giants *Eobasileus* and *Uintatherium*, soon extinct, and *Eohippus*, the first horse. Giant birds such as 7-foot-high *Diatryma* were perhaps the mammals' greatest rivals.

Mammals of the Oligocene. Above is **Brontops**, weak-brained giant, and under him an early rabbit scampers. At far left is piglike **Archaeotherium**, and behind him a herd of early **Oreodon**. Beyond **Brontops'** shoulder, in rear centre, run two **Mesohippus**, collie-sized horses. On the rocks stands a six-horned, deerlike cud-chewer, **Protoceras;** below him we see **Hyaenodon**, an early meat-eater, working over his prey. In the

TIME OF TRIAL AND TRIUMPH

The Oligocene was a time of further change. Mountain-building was widespread: the Alps pushed up; the crust of Asia began to buckle to form the Himalayas; volcanoes spewed fire and

ash over much of what is now the northwest United States, and built up mountainous cones. And in America's heartland the ancient subtropical forests retreated, while conifers and hardwood trees took over.

In the animal kingdom most of the primitive

foreground, right, is one of the first rhinoceroses, **Subhyracodon,** about to drink, while **Bothⁱiodon,** perhaps the ancestor of the hippos, wallows among the lily pads. On the bank the first tapir, **Protapirus,** hunts for grubs while a hungry **Hoplophoneus,** first of the powerful cats, armed with 2-inch fangs and retractible claws, watches him. The graceful grass-eaters in the shade at the right are early camels: **Poëbrotherium.**

mammals faded away during the Oligocene; and most of the modern families became established. Only a few of the earliest lines lingered on—as they still do—unchanged. Among these are the opossums, hedgehogs, moles, and shrews.

Rodents continued to spread; gophers, rats,

and mice appeared. And rabbits were multiplying as rapidly as they do today.

There were some new giants, too. The little horselike *Paleosyops* (the larger of the two animals at lower right, p. 88) developed into the 14-foot *Brontops,* hoofed and horned, but with

Miocene mammals. Along the bog waddle amphibious **Promerycochoerus** and **Merycoch-oerus**; the rhinos **Diceratherium** are behind them. Next are clumsy, horselike **Moropus;**

weak teeth and a brain only the size of an orange.

Of the primitive meat-eaters only *Hyaenodon* and his kin survived; but dogs, perhaps hunting in packs, and cats, each stalking alone, were now appearing on the scene. A powerful early cat was saber-toothed *Hoplophoneus.*

The hoofed vegetarians had divided into two groups—even- and odd-toed. The odd-toed included horses (then the size of collies), asses, zebras, rhinos, and tapirs. Even-toed vegetarians were cattle, sheep, goats, pigs, hippos, antelopes, camels, giraffes, and deer.

GOLDEN AGE ON THE PLAINS

The sudden spreading of the grasses in the Miocene period was a great milestone in the story of life. Having long grown in the shade of subtropical forests, the grasses were spurred by the cooler, drier climate, and created vast plains and prairies. The early grasses—ancestors of today's cereals and fodder crops—were harsh and stubbly; but as they spread across the flatlands of America, grazing animals multiplied, and many forest-dwellers moved out onto the sunny plains.

Dinohyus, piglike giant; and, in back, Machairodus, cats. To their right are a herd of Merychippus, horses; in front, four-horned Syndyoceras; then two camels, Procamelus and

Hoofed animals developed rapidly. The horse *Merychippus* grew to the height of a pony, slim and graceful. Related animals were the small rhino *Diceratherium*, the clumsy, claw-footed, horselike *Moropus*, water-loving *Promerycochoerus* and *Merycochoerus*, and plains-dwelling *Merychyus*, all doomed to disappear. There was a piglike giant, *Dinohyus*, 6 feet tall and almost as massive as a hippopotamus. The two models of camels were small, familiar-looking *Procamelus*, and *Alticamelus*, a sort of super-camel with a neck as long as a giraffe's.

Deer had experimental models, too. Long-nosed *Syndyoceras* was overburdened with two sets of horns, one on his nose, the other in front of his ears. Tiny *Merycodus*, with branching horns—he was the ancestor of pronghorn antelopes—and graceful *Cranioceras* were other deer.

Plentiful grass-eaters meant good eating for meat-eaters—weasels, martens, fishers, wolverines, skunks, and others. Raccoons and bears developed from early doglike species. In the tall grasses large cats such as *Machairodus* hunted.

During the Miocene a stranger wandered into

Alticamelus. Cattle-like group are **Merychyus**, soon to disappear. Elephant-like Mastodons are **Gomphotherium.** In right front are deer-like animals, **Cranioceras** and little **Merycodus.**

America—the long-trunked, heavy-tusked mastodon, *Gomphotherium,* from Egypt. In an ages-long journey, one of the longest in the history of life, it came across southern Asia, north to the Arctic, and across a land bridge at the Bering Straits into the New World.

THE COMING OF THE COLD

In the Pliocene period, which ended perhaps a million years ago, the winds were growing sharper. The cruel ice sheets were to come. Grasses grew shorter; forests of the Southwest dried up as the Sierra Nevada range rose. Pine trees on the northern mountains crowded out the sequoias.

Now there were many new mammals. An amphibious rhino arrived from Asia—*Teleoceras.* Largest mastodon was the big shoveltusker, *Amebelodon,* which probably scooped up roots with its huge teeth. There was a giant bear, *Agriotherium;* a huge dog, *Amphicyon;* and the only horned rodent, *Epigaulus.* Still developing were the horse, *Pliohippus,* now nearly the size of our

Pliocene and Pleistocene mammals. First of the giant mammals were the Pliocene rhino **Teleoceras** (left) and shovel-tusked mastodon, **Amebelodon.** Giant bear, **Agriotherium,** and giant dog, **Amphicyon,** are in foreground with (left) horned rodent **Epigaulus.** Behind are **Pliohippus,** near-horse, and **Synthetoceras,** a

horse today; a sturdy pronghorn, *Sphenophalos;* and an "almost-unicorn"—*Synthetoceras,* last descendant of four-horned *Syndyoceras.*

Life was flourishing as the Pliocene closed. But a crisis brought in the Pleistocene: the ice.

Vast ice sheets grew out from the north and south poles. Greenland, Siberia, and northern Europe were covered. As the sheets spread, accumulating the snows of innumerable winters, so much of the earth's moisture was trapped in ice that the level of the oceans fell. The long-sunken Isthmus of Panama was thrust up again. A land

near-unicorn. By the Pleistocene, giants were the rule—giant beaver, **Castoroides,** lower left corner; mastodon and huge woolly mammoth; **Teratornis,** biggest of flying birds, above their heads; hoofed giants, as musk ox and **Bison Crassicornis;** great wolf, **Canis dirus,** front; big sabre-toothed cat, **Smilodon,** behind.

bridge stretched from Alaska to Siberia. Animals of Asia and of North and South America streamed across these bridges. Between the Americas there was much intermingling and competition among living things. Many animal families disappeared.

In the first 100,000 years of the Pleistocene, the ice sheets covered as much as a third of the earth's land area. Then they receded, and moderate climates returned. Four times the North American glacier crunched down from the north; four times it withdrew. The latest retreat began some 10,000 years ago and is still going on.

The sabre-toothed cat, *Smilodon,* was larger and heavier than any tiger of today. Its great jaws, opening a full quarter circle, were armed with 6-inch fangs. *Teratornis,* a carrion-eating cousin of the modern condor, had a wingspread of 12 feet.

Hoofed giants included *Bison crassicornis* and the hardy musk ox of today's Arctic. The horse, *Equus,* grew to the size we know; then it died out in America, not to return until the Spanish brought in its descendants four centuries ago.

Mightiest were the mastodons and mammoths. The mammoths were recent arrivals from Asia. Of the four species, one, the woolly mammoth, stood 10 feet high. He lived around the glaciers and died among them in such numbers that his tusks have furnished half our ivory.

Up from the south came *Boreostracon,* related to the armadillos, armoured from nose to tail. The ground sloth *Mylodon* ate from trees. *Megatherium,* also a sloth, and one of the largest mammals ever, carried his witless head 20 feet high.

The Pleistocene giants died out as swiftly as the dinosaurs, and as mysteriously. As the million-year winter of the Ice Ages waned, these animals vanished from the temperate zones. Only in tropical Africa and Asia have a few survived —the elephants, rhinos, and tapirs.

Again we ask, what happened? The answer may lie in changes of climate, competition, new conditions. Man with his bone and flint weapons has been blamed, too.

But life goes on; gaps are filled. The world today is as crowded with life as ever, and has more different species. Some forms seem to go on, unchanging—opossums, oysters, rabbits, and turtles, for example. But in general the main line of animal development seems to be in those types that have greater sensitivity and greater ability to deal with changing environments. Better vision and hearing, more sensitive nervous systems, larger and more complex brains—these win out over sabre teeth and armour plate. It was this equipment, in fact, that gave the ancestors of man, back in the dim days of the Eocene, a growing advantage among the multitude of living things.

As the ice ground across the plains, rounding valleys and creating new lakes and rivers in an icy world, only animals with great vigor could endure. Among them were a beaver, *Castoroides,* the size of a small bear of today, and a 6-foot wolf, *Canis dirus,* that ranged from coast to coast.

In a coral glade off Bermuda, gorgeously coloured fish hover among exotic plants that rise from the shallow sea floor. At the extreme lower left the waving tentacles of an anemone barely enter the picture. In right foreground a pink squirrel fish—so called because it chatters like a squirrel—nuzzles a cluster of Alcyonarian corals. Above it hovers an angel fish; above that a spotted chub. In the background swim several sergeant-majors. At right is a blue-striped grunt, which does grunt. Many fish and invertebrates make noises.

PART VII

CREATURES OF THE SEA

THE CRADLE OF LIFE

As WE READ earlier, the first home of living things was the sea. The sea spawned not only the multitudes of animals that continue to dwell there, but also those that went ashore and became creatures of field, forest, and desert.

But in the sea, still, are members of all branches of life, except birds, amphibians, and true spiders. Age after age, little changed, they live on in the calm, underwater world: jellyfish and corals, glass sponges and starfish, sand dollars and horseshoe crabs and clams.

Fishes were latecomers; they were swimmers. Swimming helped them escape their enemies and keep their balance and position in the water. The outlines of fishes became streamlined, their fins flexible; they developed the movable jaws and teeth of hunters. Sharks, skates, and rays developed skeletons of soft cartilage. Others, the true fish (teleosts)—the cod, herring, salmon, tuna, mackerel, bass, and others—developed skeletons of bone. Today there are 20,000 species of true fishes in the seas.

The climate of the sea has no freezing winter blizzards or scorching summer droughts. Even in the tropics, water temperatures seldom go above 85°F.; in the polar regions, never much below 29°. Over more than three quarters of the ocean, temperatures vary less than 5° from one season to the next; below 800 feet there is no seasonal change at all.

The creatures of the sea are constantly bathed in the principal thing they need for life—water. They take water directly into their systems, getting from it the gases they need—oxygen and carbon dioxide—and also some of the salts and minerals necessary for growth.

Water supports its creatures against the tug of gravity. Sea plants need no heavy stems or tree trunks to hold them up; sea animals need no strong leg bones to stand on. The bones even of the great 140-ton whales are spongy and filled with oil. If a whale is washed ashore, it quickly dies, even though it is an air-breathing mammal, because its lungs are crushed by the weight of its body, away from the supporting water.

Thus the sea is friendly toward life—yet makes life depend upon it in peculiar ways. Sea creatures remain generally more primitive than life on land, because they have not had to develop forms to meet constantly changing conditions. Sea life depends on steady conditions of temperature, saltiness of the water, pressure, and light.

Cold-water creatures cannot live if a shift in currents brings warm water into their region. Heavy rains and floods of fresh water can kill many near-shore invertebrates by lessening the saltiness of the water.

Pressure, too, divides the sea into layers of life. The greater the depth at which an animal lives, the greater the pressure of the water on its body. Whales and some fish can move from one pressure level to another without injury, but most sea creatures must stay within certain limits.

Light is essential to all the sea plants that make up the basic food supply of the sea. Most plants convert water, carbon dioxide, and certain minerals and salts into food for their own growth. They do this by means of the energy of the sun, in the process called photosynthesis.

Sunlight does not reach deep into the water. In the depths the only light is the soft glow that some creatures themselves create. So the plants in the ocean are confined to the upper, sunlit layers. No plants grow deeper than 350 feet down.

FREE SWIMMERS OF THE OPEN SEA

Among large animals, the open waters are the home of vertebrate fish especially, though some invertebrates like the giant squid and some mammals like the mighty whale live there too. The free swimmers move lightly through a world in which swiftness, keen senses, and protective colouration are the keys to survival.

Kings of speed are the blue marlin, capable of spurts up to 50 miles per hour; the sailfish; the dolphin; and the dolphin's favourite prey, the flying fish, which taxis at 35 miles per hour and soars rather than flies through the air. Not much slower are tuna and oceanic bonito.

Most surface-dwelling fish have been tinted by nature to blend with their surroundings. Dominant colours are green, blue, and violet. Sea creatures in the sunlit upper levels are often bluish above and silver underneath. From about 600 to 1,500 feet, a twilight greyish zone, the fish are

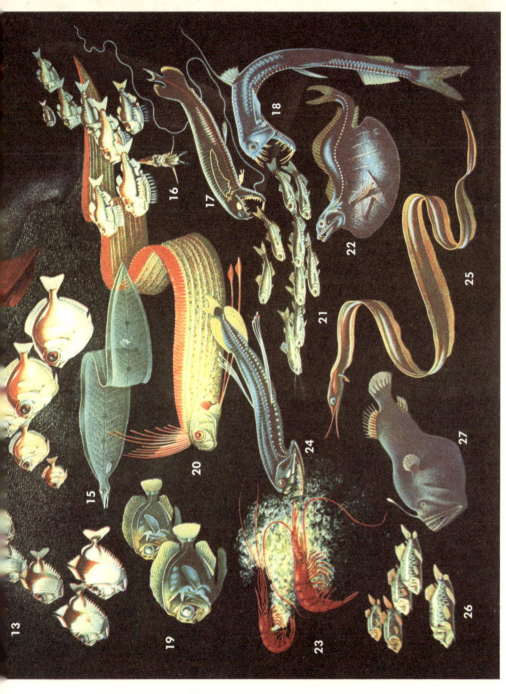

Levels of life are shown in this panoramic picture, ranging from the blue, sunlit upper regions of the sea to the dim middle world and the black depths where the light comes only from the bodies of the animals themselves. The key here identifies the animals pictured by number, with approximate lengths. 1. Blue marlin, 10 ft. 2. Flying fish, 9 in. 3. Manta, 20 ft. 4. Sailfish, 8 ft. 5. Dolphin, 4 ft. 6. Pilot fish, 9 in. 7. Sunfish, 7 ft. 8. Oceanic Bonito, 2 ft. 9. White-tipped shark, 7 ft. 10. Bluefin tuna, 7 ft. 11. Sperm whale, 60 ft. 12. Giant squid, 55 ft. 13. Sternoptyx diaphana, 2 in. 14. Diretmus argenteus, 2 in. 15. Eel larva, 4 in. 16. Hatchet fish, 1 in. 17. Lamprotoxus flagellibarba, 8 in. 18. Viperfish, 12 in. 19. Platyberix opalescens, 3 in. 20. Rooster fish, 15 ft. 21. Lantern fish, 3 in. 22. Chiasmodon niger, 2 in. 23. Prawns, 4 in. 24. Photostomias guernei, 7 in. 25. Snipe eel, 2 ft. 26. Opisthoproctus soleatus, 1 in. 27. Melanocetus Johnsoni, 2 in.

correspondingly light-hued, like silvery *Sternoptyx*, *Diretmus*, and *Opisthoproctus*. Below, in the zone of utter blackness, animals display the brown and black shades of *Melanocetus* and *Photostomias*, though a few, such as the scarlet deep-sea prawns, wear bright colours—which cannot be seen anyway!

Even in the depths, few fish are blind. Between 800 and 1,500 feet, many have enlarged eyes, sensitive to very dim light. Innumerable sea creatures glow, some with lights they can turn on and off at will; and in the hunt for food, the ability of a fish to see this glow is doubtless a real advantage.

Most deep-sea fish are equipped also with enormous mouths and long, needle-sharp teeth. One, *Chiasmodon*, has a stretchable stomach so that it can swallow prey larger than itself.

The greatest battles of the deep are those waged a quarter of a mile down by the sperm whale and its familiar prey, the giant squid (pictured here).

101

In the pastures of the sea these tiny creatures and countless others swarm by the millions, ready food for larger creatures. At left, lower middle, is a pick-shaped dinoflagellate. Above is a copepod, to its right, a shrimp-like mysid. Sea worms, one with two egg sacs, are in the upper left corner. A "flying" snail

PLANTS OF THE SEA

Nowhere beneath the waters is plant life so thick as in forests on the land. Undersea mountains are bleaker than storm-swept peaks; the great plains and valleys of the ocean floor are more barren than the desert. Where there is plant life, it is primitive—rootless, trunkless, generally small and limited in kind.

There are only a few seed plants, such as eel

grass and surf grass. The rest are seaweeds, tiny blue-green algae, and the single-celled plants called diatoms (shown right, above).

Diatoms can be seen by humans only through a microscope; but they reproduce faster than any plants on land. In spring and fall the surface of the sea turns yellow, brown, and green with diatoms. They thrive in cold water, where the rich minerals and salts from the ocean floor are swept upward on deep currents. And hordes of sea crea-

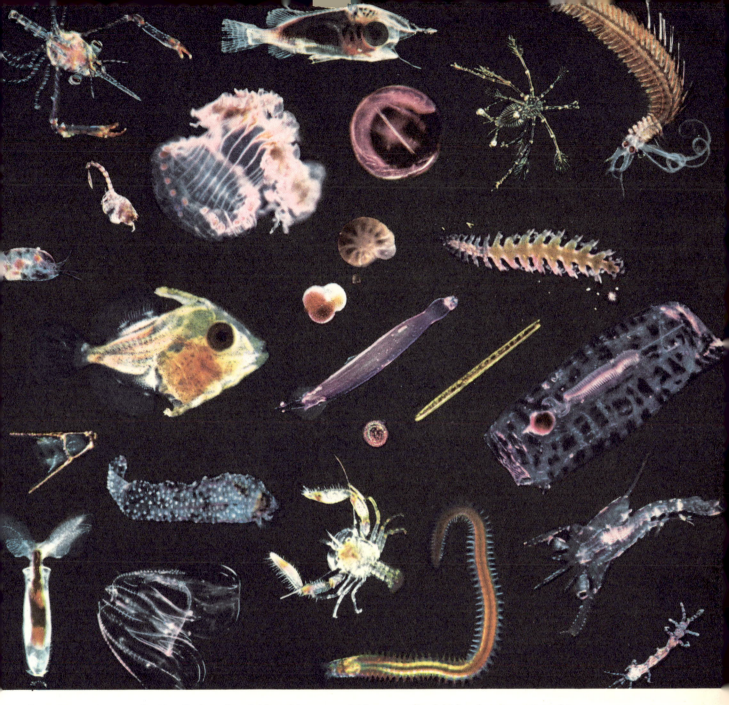

is at top centre; sea "spiders" at centre right and in upper right corner. On right-hand page, near centre, is a straight yellow diatom. To left, small circles are radiolarians and foraminifera. A sea worm with tentacles is in the upper right corner, with a sea spider to its left. Young fishes appear at left and top centre.

tures swarm through the diatom pastures to feed.

Where diatoms flourish, the world's great fisheries are found—along the west coasts of North and South America, in the North Sea, off Portugal, Japan, and Newfoundland.

THE PASTURES OF THE SEA

One of the most important and far-flung kinds of life in the sea is plankton. It is not a single kind of life but a floating community of both plants and animals, found in surface waters. Most are tiny, even microscopic. There are diatoms and other one-celled plants, and slightly larger animals that feed on the plants and spend all their lives floating on the waters.

Thousands upon thousands of different species—various larvae, minute shelled animals, sea worms and sea "spiders," baby fish, and others—make up a plankton community. None of these

103

creatures can swim against the currents. They simply drift.

Plankton is the basic food supply of the sea. For in the sea, as on land, animals depend on plants for food. Only the plants can change simple substances into the sugars, starches, and proteins that nourish animals. So the tiniest animals feed on the diatoms, which make up six tenths of plankton. And larger animals feed on the smaller.

THE ENDLESS CYCLE OF FOOD

Save for those small animals that graze on diatoms, every free-swimming creature lives on the flesh of others smaller than itself. And it in turn is food for others larger.

Copepods, for example, are among the most important food animals. These tiny animals, ranging from pinhead size to a quarter of an inch, eat the microscopic diatoms. Baby herrings eat copepods by the thousands. But squids, like many other sea creatures (and man too), enjoy herring.

Catching a fish in its tentacles, the squid with its horny, parrot-like beak bites out big chunks, and down goes herring into squid. Then along comes a bass and eats the squid. Finally the adult sea bass—weighing perhaps 6 pounds, and about 18 inches long—unless it becomes prey itself, will eventually die and sink to the bottom, there to be eaten or to decompose into fertilizer for the diatoms. So the cycle starts again.

About 10 pounds of food is required to build one pound of the animal that eats it. Thus it would take 10,000 pounds of diatoms to make 1,000 pounds of copepods to make 100 pounds of herring to make 10 pounds of squid to make one pound of bass to make 1/10 pound of man.

All the creatures mentioned above—that is, both plankton and nekton (all the free swimmers)—belong to the pelagic (open-water) branch of sea life. The other branch of marine life is called benthic, or bottom-dwelling. It includes the shallow, inshore sea bottoms and the deep-sea floors beyond the continental slopes as well. It is a very different domain of life, as we shall now see.

Hanging gardens of sea plants provide pasturage or hunting grounds for many small creatures like this halfbeak under sargassum weed in the Caribbean Sea.

The endless chain of food.

1. Copepod eats diatoms.
2. Herring eats copepods.
3. Squid eats herring.
4. Bass eats squid. Man eats bass or bass dies, decays, and provides nourishment for diatoms.

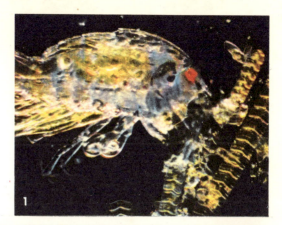

THE BOTTOM DWELLERS

In the shallows near shore lie weedy gardens where life flourishes as nowhere else in the sea. Here on the pale sands and mud live a multitude of sluggish creatures in a slow-motion world.

Many seem more like plants than animals, and look so much like plants that they have been given plant-like names: sea anemones, sea cucumbers, sea peaches, sea grapes. Yet they are animals—soft-bodied invertebrates well adapted to life on the ocean floor.

Many of them are motionless, "fixed" creatures like the sponges and corals. Their major problem is finding a place to attach themselves.

Every rock, every bit of sand or mud, has its tenants—creeping, crawling, or stationary. There are barnacles, mussels, oyster drills, sea vases, sponges, and pink-hearted hydroids attached to wooden pilings (as in the picture above). An empty snail shell may be taken over for protection by a soft-backed hermit crab; a sea anemone may even fasten itself on top.

Even beneath the surface of the sand there are many homes—the mazes of sea worms, the holes of moon shells, the burrows of fiddler crabs which venture out at low tide to search for food, the hideaways of razor clams.

This is a world built upon the rich supply of minerals dissolved in the water and stored on

Bottom-dwellers 1. Sea Colander **2.** Phyllaria Dermatodea Seaweed **3.** Mussel Shell **4.** Sea Grapes **5.** Edible Mussels **6.** Pink Hearted Hydroids **7.** Red-beard Sponge **8.** Ribbed Mussels **9.** Common Starfish **10.** Razor Clam Shell **11.** Oyster Drills **12.** Rock Barnacles **13.** Irish Moss **14.** Sea Vases **15.** Sea Anemone, retracted **16.** Sea Pork **17.** Sun Star **18.** Moon Snail Shell **19.** Boat Shell **20.** Dog Whelks **21.** Periwinkles **22.** Purple Starfish **23.** Coralline Algae **24.** Blood Starfish **25.** Sand Dollar and Shell **26.** Mud Star **27.** Brittle Star **28.** Rockweed **29.** Rock Crab **30.** Green Sea Urchin and Shell **31.** Sea Peaches **32.** Bay Scallop Shell **33.** Jingle Shells **34.** Green Crab **35.** Sea Anemone, expanded **36.** Hermit Crab in his borrowed shell **37.** Soft Coral **38.** Sea Cucumber **39.** Whelk Egg Cases **40.** Skate Egg Capsule **41.** Purple Sea Urchin **42.** Kelp **43.** Sea Anemone **44.** Blue Crab **45.** Lady Crab **46.** Horseshoe Crab **47.** Tortoiseshell Limpets **48.** Clathria Delicata Sponge **49.** Eyed Finger Sponge

the ocean floor. These creatures depend especially on calcium, which builds their hard shells and strong pincers and gives them anchorage for their muscles for digging and clinging and crawling. In the tropics, where calcium is absorbed more readily than in cold water, one of the large species of clam grows shells weighing as much as 500 pounds.

The minerals of the bottom are important also to the plant life which flourishes in these sea gardens—the rockweed, kelp, and Irish moss. Though they are rootless, large seaweeds must be anchored. They fasten themselves to rocks or sand by threadlike "holdfasts" or flat discs. And if their anchorage lies deep, they may put out stems up to 100 feet long so that their main foliage can float in sunlight, held up by little self-contained bulbs of gas.

The largest of the seaweeds are the kelps. These flat, brown plants anchor in rocky areas off-shore beyond the zone of crashing surf, to depths of 100 feet. Although these larger seaweeds are harvested by man for his chemical industries, few marine animals, except the sea hare, browse directly on them. But some of the smaller algae, which grow like a furry slime on rocks and other sunken objects, provide food for certain crabs and shrimps and many sharp-tongued snails and other creatures of this strange sea-bottom world.

Sea squirts cluster in inch-high colonies over rocks and pilings. They feed by pumping water in and out of their two body-openings. When alarmed, these creatures squirt water from both holes.

Serpent stars (below) eat mollusks and slime. They crawl along the bottom, mouth down, for food. If cut in half, each half becomes a complete animal.

LAZY HUNTERS OF THE OCEAN FLOOR

Many sea creatures do not go hunting for food. They simply open their mouths—if they have mouths—and suck in the sea water. From it they strain out the food particles as they go by. In open water these particles are plankton. On the bottom there is a kind of slime composed of decaying matter and the bacteria that break it down, as well as swarms of tiny living things.

Sponges and sea squirts anchor themselves to rocks or other solid objects and feed by pumping water in and out of their openings. Oysters and clams are pumpers too, and the oysters spend their whole adult lives quietly in beds.

The sea anemone here has paralysed a small fish with the poisoned "needles" in the whitish spirals around its tentacles. When the fish becomes helpless, it is drawn into the anemone's mouth.

The file shell has dozens of little blue or red "eyes." Its tentacles are sensitive to taste and to touch. It feeds by forcing water through its layers of scarlet gills to strain out the food particles.

Some organisms make a little more effort. Barnacles catch food bits in the bristles of their outstretched hairy legs. Sea cucumbers snuffle along the sea floor like vacuum cleaners, shovelling slime into their mouths with tentacles. They may cover 18 inches a day.

The sea anemone looks like a flower but actually is a meat-eating animal. By means of a slimy disc on its underside, it clings to rocks or glides along the bottom. It catches small fish in its stinging tentacles, then draws the paralysed prey into its mouth.

One large free swimmer which comes down to the bottom to feed is the eagle ray, which uses its wide, wing-like fins to stir up the sand in search of mollusks. As it digs it scoops up the clams and crushes them between its rows of flat teeth.

The sea urchin has this mouth on its underside. The mouth is armed with five efficient "teeth" which can crush small shellfish, cut up sea lettuce (a seaweed), and scrape algae off the rocks.

The pipefish can hardly be seen among the blades of eel-grass. This camouflage protects it while it probes with long snout for the shrimps and other small creatures that it seeks for its dinner.

THE ARTS OF DEFENCE AND CAMOUFLAGE

In a world of hungry hunters, each species must work out its own means of defence and attack. Some, like the tuna, shark, and barracuda, have the implements of sheer power—sharp teeth, swift reflexes, speed and strength. The sawfish waves before him a long saw-nose, equipped with two rows of bony "teeth." He swims into a school of smaller fish and hacks them to pieces.

The slow-moving snails, clams, and oysters try to escape their foes by retreating into their shells.

Some creatures have special and unusual defences. Squid, octopi, and some shrimp blind their enemies by discharging dark "ink" into the water around them.

Jellyfish and sea anemones have coiled, hollow darts with which they can inject poison to paralyse their attackers. Sting rays have poisoned spines on their tails; other rays and some eels can give electric shocks. Sponges lodge tiny spikes in their enemies.

Certain sea cucumbers can cast off some of

The blowfish of the coral seas inflates itself with water when foes approach. At the same time its spines, which normally lie flat against its body, rise up, so that the animal looks to its enemies like a too-large, very unappetising meal.

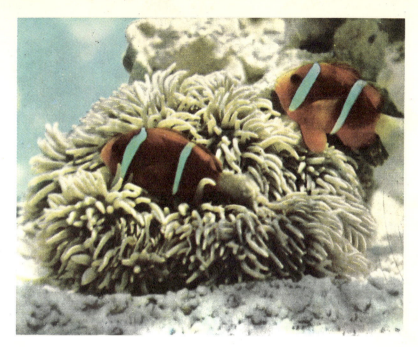

Damselfish wait among the tentacles of a sea anemone. They are mysteriously safe from the poisoned sting of the tentacles. But they lure larger fish, which the anemone kills and which they share.

their insides. While the enemy pauses over these, the cucumber escapes. Later it grows new parts.

Flatfish, rackfish, and pipefish, living among the eel-grass and seaweed groves of the shallows close to shore, have forms and colours that make them hard to see among the grass blades.

Decorator crabs cement bits of seaweed over their shells and legs. The hermit crab, which has a tender rump, shields it by living in a discarded shell. Among such slow-moving creatures, defence is—next to food—the most important part of life.

MOVING ABOUT

Air is so easy to move through that we are scarcely aware of it; but sea creatures have to use a great deal of energy to force their way through the water. They have many ways of getting themselves about.

Not all creatures of the sea swim, by any means. Plankton, as we have seen, simply drifts. Some bottom creatures—corals, sponges, and oysters—do not move at all. Most bottom creatures, though, walk; crabs and lobsters crawl on jointed

A squirting sea hare defends itself by ejecting "ink." This mollusk is named for its long, rabbit-ear-like antennae (at left). Ink from a related mollusk gave the ancient Phoenicians Tyrian purple.

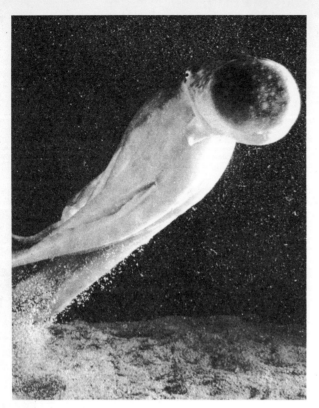

Jet-propelled is the octopus, which fills a thick, muscular mantle with water, then thrusts it out through a funnel that can be turned in any direction. When on the sea bottom, the octopus crawls on its tentacles. Contrary to the popular stories, it is rarely, if ever, dangerous to man.

Walking on the ocean floor is possible for the batfish, which has fins that resemble legs. The tail is for swimming.

legs; snails and anemones glide on slimy feet. There is even a fish, the West Indian batfish, which can use its fins as legs to walk across the ocean floor. The horseshoe crab swims, crawls on the bottom, and floats on its back, using its legs as oars.

The swimmers are mainly fishes and marine mammals—whales, porpoises, and seals. Most fishes push themselves along with sidewise movements of body and tail, and sometimes by forcing water out through their gills. They steer and brake with their fins. But the eagle ray "flies" through the water, flapping its great fins like wings.

Fish navigate by eyesight, hearing (through cells along the sides of their bodies), touch, and smell. But how fish swim in formation—twisting, diving, accelerating in unison, yet never colliding —is a mystery.

Another mystery is how fish rest. They have no eyelids, and some must keep in motion to stay above the bottom. Some flatfish of the sea bottoms, like flounders, soles, skates, and rays, often do lie down on the mud. Others wedge themselves into cracks in rocks for rest. Some seem to float among drifting seaweed. But as to the free swimmers, no one can say how they sleep or if they rest at all.

LIFE AND DEATH IN THE SEA

Fish lay eggs at an unbelievable rate. If every codfish egg laid in the sea grew into an adult fish, in six years the Atlantic Ocean would be packed solid with cod. A female codfish may lay up to 5 million eggs at a time, an oyster 11 million, a sunfish 300 million. Yet life in the sea is so hazardous that the miracle is not the vast numbers of eggs laid but that any survive at all.

Only a few sea creatures, such as the octopus, care for their eggs. In most cases the eggs are discharged freely into the water, to drift with the currents or settle to the bottom, taking their chances among numberless hungry hunters. Some

An eagle ray, flapping its huge fins, "flies" through the water like a great bird of prey. It is about 4 feet wide from fin-tip to fin-tip.

eggs hatch into larvae, and from these develop little fish. These, too, are lucky to survive.

Sometimes the development from egg to adult fish covers not only several years but many miles of travel. Perhaps the greatest of all travelers is the European eel. Each autumn, adult eels leave their fresh-water homes, make their way to the sea, then somehow cross 3,000 miles of the Atlantic to their spawning grounds in the weedy Sargasso Sea. Here they lay their eggs, and from here the eel larvae start their long journey home in the swirl of the Gulf Stream. The journey north and east to Europe takes three years. At its end the larvae turn into elvers, swim upstream to the rivers and lakes, and there develop into adult eels. Ten years later they return to the sea, to lay their eggs and die.

So Nature works out a wonderful balance between destruction and lavish reproduction, and each species is carried on.

And some day from the riches of the sea may come the answer to the old problem of human hunger. Some day we may learn to harvest the meadows of plankton, and to use the algae and diatoms, those most prolific of all plants, for the nourishment of man.

Jumping file shell stirs up sand by clapping its shells.

PART VIII

THE CORAL REEF

WHAT ARE CORAL ISLES?

EVER SINCE European explorers began to rove the tropic oceans, the Western world has heard tales of coral isles, palm-fringed and surf-ruffled, of island necklaces ringing turquoise lagoons. Below the surface of the waters men glimpsed a fabulous world of living creatures more colourful than any on land. This was the magic realm of flower-like animals, giant clams and fish with scales flashing gold and silver, ruby and emerald, glinting among the grottoes of coral gardens.

Not many years ago, men learned what coral really is. Now we know that the substance we call coral is composed of the skeletons of innumerable tiny marine animals. Flourishing in all the world's warm waters, these creatures have built thousands of reefs, atolls, and islands, including one of the greatest structures ever built by living beings—the Great Barrier Reef of Australia.

Because of the blossom-like appearance of coral gardens, corals were long mistaken for plants. But they belong to the same section of the animal kingdom as jellyfish and sea anemones. An individual coral polyp (animal) is little more than a cylinder or tube ridged inside with spokelike partitions. At the top is a mouth, bearded with tentacles which look much like flower petals. This simple opening serves as an inlet for food and an outlet for wastes, sperm, and eggs. At the other end of the tube is a round foot anchored to a limy cup, which rests in turn on some solid object. Usually this solid base is made up of the skeletons of former generations.

Star-coral skeletons mesh like cogwheels to form reefs.

Organ-pipe-coral polyps built these empty pipelike houses.

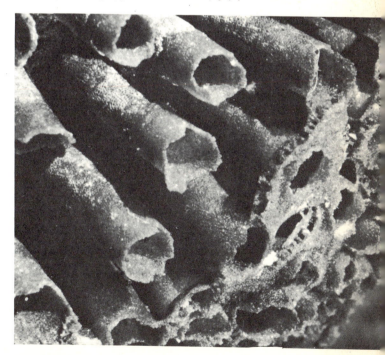

The reef builders (opposite page) of the Bahamas, living coral polyps, here emerge at night from their pale stone mansions to feed in the phosphorescent waters. In the middle of the colony a tubeworm waves his feathery gills.

A barrier reef. At the left of the reef is the 600-foot-deep open sea; at right is a quiet, shallow channel sheltered by the reef. The surf crashes against the under-water coral cliffs. On this side coral polyps keep building, age after age, upward and outward toward sunlight and the open sea.

Coral grows in all seas, but the reef-building varieties are found only in shallow, sunlit, tropical waters—never deeper than 150 feet, rarely at temperatures below 68°F., seldom more than 1,500 miles from the equator.

Corals must have sunlight for the algae which mysteriously grow in their tissues. They must have clean water; sediment and mud suffocate them. Moving water is needed to bring them sufficient food and oxygen. They are flesh-eaters, feeding on young fish, tiny shelled creatures, and sea worms, which they catch with stinging tentacles.

As larvae they swim about briefly, then settle down, usually in a coral colony. They start secreting lime and quickly build up a cuplike armour for protection. It is the labour of untold generations of small workers that has reared up the

An atoll. Here an island sank, and as it sank, a ring of coral grew upward and outward from it. The water in the centre, over the sunken island, is less than 200 feet deep. From the windward side (foreground of the picture) surf foams over the coral wall into the central lagoon. Toward the leeward side in the distance a small island has been formed of old coral shells ground into sands by millions of years of wave action.

Fringing reefs surround old volcanic islands. Here the coral has built outward from the solid rock shores of the island, again toward the open sea. If the island should sink entirely, the coral would continue to grow upward and outward, forming around the site of the island an atoll (see below).

coral islands, reefs, and atolls of the oceans as we know them today.

Three typical creations of coral are the fringing reef, the barrier reef, and the atoll.

Fringing reefs are those that fan out from the edge of land in an almost solid shelf. The barrier reef is separated from land by a wide lagoon or channel. The atoll, built out from a sunken island, is a coral ring enclosing a lagoon in the open sea.

The rock under some atolls extends 4,000 feet down into the sea. Countless generations of coral have built a mighty tower there, shell by tiny shell.

Great coral reefs are found not only in modern seas but in many land areas that were under water millions of years ago. A great series of coral reefs, formed in the Paleozoic Era, has been discovered in western Canada.

Three kinds of reefs shown on these pages are the principal kinds which make up the Great Barrier Reef of Australia, largest coral structure in modern oceans (described on pages 118-119).

BUNKER GROUP

CAPRICORN GROUP

MACKAY

TOWNSVILLE

HINCHINBROOK IS.

FLINDERS PASSAGE

WHITSUNDAY PASSAGE

SWAIN REEFS

N

South Pacific Ocean

The Great Barrier Reef runs 1,260 miles along the northeast coast of Australia.

THE GREAT BARRIER REEF OF AUSTRALIA

One of the greatest structures ever built is this series of coral reefs, 1,260 miles long and 500 feet high. The outer edge is 7 miles from the mainland in some places, as much as 100 miles in others. On the seaward side the coral walls fall away steeply to depths as great as 8,000 feet. But the huge lagoon inside the great reef is shallow, seldom more than 120 feet deep. This lagoon is calm, for the coral cliffs—though some never rise above the surface—protect it from the violence of the ocean waves, which break in surf outside.

These calm waters, called Australia's "grand canal," are travelled by coastal ships. But the waters are dotted with numberless islands, atolls, and uncharted coral outcroppings. It takes an experienced sailor to pick his way through them.

The islands close to the mainland, within the sheltering wall of the reef (shown dark on the map), were once the high points of a part of the Australian coastal plain, which in ages past was submerged. The warm, shallow waters along the sinking coastline favoured coral. Colonies sprang up all along the now-sunken shore. Perhaps at the rate of 3 feet every 1,000 years, the coral grew upward and outward toward the sea as the coastal plain settled down.

GROWTH AND DESTRUCTION

In coral reefs, the limy skeletons of corals are the main building blocks. These alone make an often quite loose honeycomb, which becomes filled with smaller shells and other debris. The resulting structure is fortified against the waves by the coralline algae, which lay down deposits of lime that act as a binding mortar.

By day and by night, while the coral polyps are building up their dwellings in many patterns,

On the seaward side its walls fall to depths as great as 8,000 feet. Inside are shallow channels.

other forces are at work tearing them down. The Trade Winds are forever hurling waves against the seaward coral walls. Typhoons break up vast sections of reef, ripping out huge blocks of coral and tumbling them across the lagoon. Tropical downpours of rain reduce the saltiness of the water and often turn a whole busy community of coral into a graveyard.

There are plant and animal enemies, too—sea urchins that rasp holes into the coral walls, mollusks and algae that bore in, clams that wedge themselves into cracks, deepening them into cavities. As everywhere in Nature, destruction goes on side by side with growth, and death with life.

CORAL ISLANDS

The forces of creation are victorious all along the Great Barrier; the corals continue to build. Today the reef is still a row of separate structures, but some day these units may be joined and built up into coral islands. For as the skeletons of the corals and other small animals of the reef crumble under the attack of the waves, they gradually form a beach. In time the sands are cemented together again with shells and coral fragments, and hardened into rock. So begins the coral island.

Seeds of grass, shrubs, or trees may be brought to the island by birds or driftwood. Coconuts can float for miles with the currents and then wash ashore and sprout; so can the seedlings of mangrove trees. And when seeds sprout and put down roots in the sand, it may not be long before the once-bare and tide-swept reef becomes a picturesque green island.

These coral islands are lovely from a distance, with leafy trees rising like plumes, and scalloped borders of sand and surf. But close up they are often less enchanting.

Tangled mangrove swamps often cover the muddy, sheltered side of the island. The man-

A lonely mangrove tree rises on a tangle of stilt-roots from the swampy waters of a Barrier Reef atoll.

may be coconut palms, banyans, *Tournefortia,* and pawpaw trees, and ferns and ironwood as well.

The pandanus trees are perhaps of most importance to human residents. The pineapple-shaped "breadfruit" can be pounded into a kind of dough, and the long, flexible leaves can be woven into house walls and roofs; so the tree provides both food and shelter. In thick groves these long, thick leaves of the pandanus, falling to the ground, choke out all other plant life.

groves are held above the swampy soil on a framework of stiltlike roots. From their branches other roots drop down into the ooze. These spreading roots collect debris and sediment, which in time build up a higher soil base, and this kills the trees that created it. Higher, drier sections of the island are often a tangle of pandanus or "breadfruit" trees, which also have many stiltlike roots. There

BIRDS OF THE REEF

Bird life thrives on the islands of the Barrier Reef. In certain months uncountable multitudes of birds dramatically appear out of the blue, lonely wastes and hang over the Barrier Islands in dark clouds, soaring, wheeling, and screeching.

Noddy terns, sooty terns, boobies, and mutton birds or shearwaters come by the millions to mate, build their nests, and rear their young. Each female lays but a single egg during the season. But they come in such numbers that the beaches are simply covered with the gleaming white shells of their eggs, and the whole island is one vast roost, cluttered with nests. As many as 143 of the rough nests of the seabirds have been counted in a single tree.

Sooty terns, most active of reef birds, promenade on an island beach of the Great Barrier Reef of Australia.

For most of the year these birds range the South Seas. But in season some instinct calls them back to the Barrier Reef. One island scarcely three miles around has a bird population of more than a million in season. By day they fly out over the waters in search of food. By night they make love, fight, and feed their young, screeching and shrieking, groaning and moaning. In the days of sailing ships a legend said that these islands were haunted by souls in torment.

The birds share their coral beaches with large populations of soldier crabs and giant green turtles. When the tide goes out at night, the beaches come alive with ranks of tiny crabs out for food, marching about like platoons of soldiers. At dawn they dig into small burrows to hide from the hunters — the birds. Meanwhile the giant green turtles have come ashore to lay their eggs. Each mother turtle plods straight up the beach, struggling awkwardly over boulders instead of going around them. Above the high tide mark she stops, digs down until her shell is level with the beach, and then scoops out behind her a hole in which she lays a hundred or so eggs of pingpong ball size. She covers them with sand, then abandons them, returning to the sea.

A few weeks later, when the baby turtles hatch, they make their way by instinct down the beach toward the sea. Not all of them reach it. For often the shadow of dark wings falls

Spiny sea urchins, protected by spines, thrive among mangrove roots. The round object near centre is a brain coral.

across them, and the strong beaks of the larger birds snatch them up, tearing their tender shells. Even those that escape the birds and reach the surf are not assured of safety, for hungry fish are waiting. Life is never safe, even on a sunny reef.

King coral is related to the red coral of the jewel trade, which is a Mediterranean variety. This is a scene in waters off New Caledonia.

ARTISTS OF THE REEFS

Beneath the surface, coral reefs all present a strange, exciting world. Here are riotously colourful gardens of stone, with many varieties of blooms and frozen flowers of every shape and colour. There are exquisitely branching trees and shrubs; there are tapered spires, fans, and fronds. They sprout from the sunlit bottoms; they cling to ledges of the seaward cliffs.

In addition to flower-like forms, there are corals that look like toadstools, others resembling human brains. Corals grow in tiers like apartment houses, hang in folds like draperies, form caves, grottoes, and strange shapes of all sorts.

In general, the main reef-building corals have six tentacles—or multiples of six. They separate into two main groups: delicate branching forms like the staghorns and unbranched, sturdier types like the "brain" corals.

Staghorn corals (left) reach toward surface in picture taken off Nassau. From left to right: sea whips (a form of coral), a trumpet fish swimming straight up, and a waving sea fan (another coral).

Reef garden (right) has red-beard sponges (upper left); speckled sea pork (centre); two starfish and two pink sea anemones (right); a spiny sea urchin (lower right corner); and pale green coral (left).

There are many varieties—the solitary, plate-sized mushroom coral; the yellow, blade-like crust of the Millepore coral; soft, eight-tentacled Alcyonarian corals which usually do not build limy skeletons; and the so-called horny Alcyonarians such as sea whips and sea fans. There are other inhabitants of coral reefs: burrowing mollusks and sponges, for example. But the corals alone are the craftsmen who create these castles of the sea. It is odd that Nature chose a creature so small to be supreme artists in her domain.

INVERTEBRATE VISITORS

Nowhere is there more life per square foot than in the waters around a coral reef. Here the primitive, soft-bodied creatures—the invertebrates—come into their own. On the coral reefs there are giant starfish a foot in diameter, anemones two feet across, seven-pound oysters, 500-pound clams.

Here the invertebrates outdo themselves in colour, too. Species that are elsewhere drab here flaunt gorgeous raiment: starfish shine in sapphire and scarlet; tiny shrimp glow with iridescent hues. Painted lobsters promenade in purple and green, orange and black, with spots on their backs and stripes down their legs. But none is handsomer or more elegant than the shy and dainty tubeworm, with its fine-feathered gills. These close like a parasol or open to steer food down to the claw-like feelers and mouth.

A **trunkfish** cannot swim like other fish—by moving the rear of its body from side to side. Its torso is rigid. Swimming is done by rapid movements of fins and tail. Here the fish swims by a coral tree.

VERTEBRATE VISITORS

Coral islands have been called "oases in a watery desert"—the desert of the open ocean. Lagoons and shallows, tidal pools and grottoes, swarm with invertebrates and fish more varied than in the sea. The clear reef waters are shallow; so the big edible fish that like colder, deep water will not be found here. But many rare, exotic species fill their place.

The four main families of the reefs are butter-flies, damsels, sturgeons, and wrasses. They can live on plant life if they need to, when living prey grows scarce. Another sizable family, the parrot fish, actually crunch and swallow coral rock to get the algae on which they live. One species of file-fish eats the coral polyps; others eat crustaceans and mollusks.

There are a few big hunters—the fierce, crafty barracuda, the amberjack, and the giant grouper, ranging up to 600 pounds. Aside from these, most reef fish tend to be small and delicate. But like

The parrot fish (left), only vertebrate of the reef that can eat and digest the hard crust of coral algae. For this it uses its horny beak and four teeth which, set deep in its throat, act as a grinding mill.

The Sargassum fish (right) is hard to see clinging to Sargassum weeds with hand-like fins. Note its ribbons, knobs, and tassels, very much like the seaweeds among which the fish hunts its prey. The Sargassum fish is a great flesh-eater.

A **frog fish** lying in wait for prey looks like an algae-covered rock. From its head dangles a movable rod with a lure to attract curious smaller fish. These soon vanish into the frog fish's big jaws.

the invertebrates with which they share this bright coral world, they are splendidly arrayed.

They are cleverly suited to their surroundings, too. The conch fish, which hides behind the shell of the big conch mollusks, is tinted to blend with that shell; the frog fish and the scorpion fish are camouflaged to look like harmless algae as they lie in wait for their prey. The Sargassum fish, clinging to the Sargassum weed with its handlike fins (below), is decorated to look like a clump of foliage itself. Hogfish and groupers change colour as they glide past varied backgrounds. Butterfly fish wear, on their tails, eye-shaped patterns which possibly confuse attackers.

There are urchin fish which live among the spines of the sea urchin, damselfish which hide among the tentacles of the sea anemone, and the tiny pearl fish, Carapus, which actually makes its home inside the body of the sea cucumber.

Many reef fish have developed special physical characteristics in adapting to their lives. Thus needlefish and certain others which hunt near

The **conch fish** is a reef dweller whose main defence is camouflage. Hiding in the shadow of the conch mollusk's shell, and tinted just the shade of the big shell's lip, this fish is quite hard for enemies to find.

A **sting ray** (at right), camouflaging itself with sand, waits for prey to swim within reach.

Urchin fish, heads down, find welcome protection among the upright spines of a sea urchin.

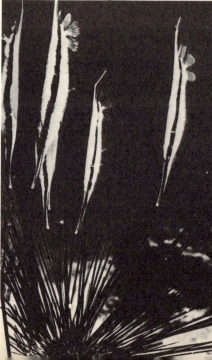

the surface have ridges over their eyes to shield them from the glaring sun. Flounders, which lie on one flat side on sandy bottoms, have mouths on one side. Even more remarkable, one eye moves, early in life, to join the other on the upward side of the flounder's face. One species of mullet has another special adaptation: thick, fleshy, fringed lips which serve to keep sand out of its mouth.

Some reef creatures are equipped with poison, too. Among these are certain sea urchins, the sting ray, and the scorpion and lionfish, whose poisonous spines can cause temporary paralysis.

Deadliest of all reef creatures is the stonefish. Thirteen spines stand up from its slimy, warty back, each needle-sharp and fed by a pair of venom glands containing a nerve poison for which there is no known antidote.

126

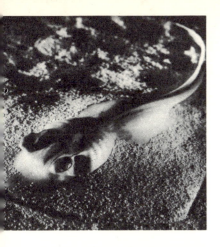

The reef fish use their poison not for attack, but only for defence. The sting ray lies on the bottom, letting sand drift over its flat, widespread "wings" to hide it. It is alert for prey; its hungry mouth is ready; but the sting in its tail will not be used unless the ray is attacked.

Only the shark, the barracuda, the moray eel, and an occasional giant grouper will attack a human visitor to the reefs. And some naturalists claim that a swimmer is safe as long as he stays under water in clear sight of the fish, instead of splashing about on the surface.

No sea monsters ready to swallow ships, like those in ancient tales, have yet been found. But year by year, as divers explore the undersea reefs, new wonders are disclosed.

The peacock worm, which is a kind of tubeworm, here extends its gills to breathe. Around its body it has built a stiff tube which it has anchored to the coral or sand. Only the animal's head sticks out of this tube. Rippling movements of the fine hairs or "feathers" on the gills send food down to the claw-like feelers and the mouth. When alarmed, the peacock worm closes its gills like parasols and withdraws into its tube.

Sand dunes shifting across a vast, lifeless plain represent the desert to many people. Actually less than 30 percent of the Sahara and only about 2 percent of the Great American Desert (pictured here) are covered with sand. In most desert regions enough rain falls so that certain plants and animals can prosper.

PART IX

THE LAND OF THE SUN

WHAT IS A DESERT?

ALL DESERTS, wherever they are, are alike in some ways. They are all lands of the sky—enormous, overpoweringly blue by day, by night a huge purple bowl sequinned with innumerable stars.

They are lands of the sun, with glaring light that seems to suck the bright colours from the earth, leaving only soft tans, grey-greens, and dull, muted reds.

They are bare lands, where the mantle of soil and green plant life that softens other scenes is worn and threadbare. Their bones lie exposed.

Most of all, they are dry lands. Dry riverbeds furrow the hills. Mud lies cracked in the beds of the empty lakes. From time to time swift winds race across the flats, raising clouds of yellow dust. But rarely do clouds drop rain.

The main characteristic of any desert is dryness. There are many ways of defining just what a desert is, but the simplest definition is any area which has an annual rainfall of less than 10 inches. It is this lack of rainfall that shapes all the other characteristics of the desert—the widely spaced plants with tiny leaves or none at all; the animals, small, burrowing creatures many of which are equipped to go through life without drinking water; the wind-worn rocks and harsh, soilless terrain. All these are shaped by lack of rain.

Deserts are not completely dry. Occasionally a sudden downpour will fill the dry stream beds with rushing torrents that roar down the parched canyons for an hour or two, then sink without a trace into the thirsty earth.

One cause of deserts is the presence of mountains between them and the sea. Here are green, wooded slopes on coastal mountainsides facing the sea. As moisture-carrying winds blow in from the sea and move up the cool mountainsides, they drop their moisture there.

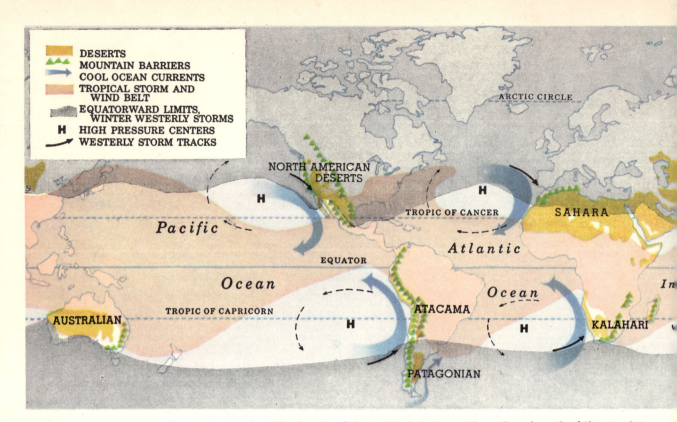

The deserts of the world circle the earth north and south of the equator.

Over most deserts there is very little moisture in the air at any time. Exceptions are the coastal "fog" deserts of South America and Africa. These have moist air, clouds, and mists but practically no rain. The Sahara, on the other hand, shows cloud cover of only 10 percent during the winter and less than 4 percent from June to October.

Deserts are the hottest places on earth. The highest temperature ever officially recorded was taken in the Sahara: 136°F. in the shade. The U. S. record is not much lower: 134° in Death Valley, California.

Because they have so little moisture in the air, deserts lose heat quickly when night comes. Days may be very warm, nights quite cold. Deserts also have wide ranges of temperature from season to season. Middle-latitude deserts like Asia's have scorching summers and freezing winters.

CAUSES OF DESERTS

The deserts of today did not always exist. Most of them developed during the last 15 million years,

as the earth's present highest mountains were being lifted up. These mountains helped cause some deserts. Moisture-laden winds lose their moisture as they move against and over cool, high ranges. Some of the rainiest regions on earth lie on the windward side of mountains, and beyond those same mountains lie deserts.

Some regions become deserts because they are far from the sea. Seacoasts are likely to be warmer than inland regions. As warm, moist winds blow inland, they tend to cool and lose moisture on the way.

The dry coastal deserts of Chile and Peru lie very near the ocean. They are deserts because of the cold Antarctic Current, which sweeps up the coast here. It chills the soft, damp Pacific breezes and condenses their moisture into fog. When this chilled, moist air rolls inland it is warmed. As warm air it can carry more moisture than before, so it blows on inland, rarely dropping rain. The Atacama Desert in South America is the driest in the world—with half an inch of rain per year—though it lies only a few miles from the sea.

The deserts of the world lie in two bands cir-

cling the globe, above and below the equator. Often they lie in the western portions of continents, where warm, dry air sweeps away the cloud cover.

America's Sonoran Desert is affected by all these causes. The coastal ranges of California and Mexico keep out moisture-bearing winds from the Pacific. The cold California current creates fog conditions along Baja (Lower) California. The interior is bathed by dry, descending air. It has the land forms typical of all deserts—bare, eroded mountains, desert flats, alluvial fans of sediment swept down the mountainsides by sudden rains, restless dunes of wind-blown sands, parched riverbeds, and dry lakes. So we shall use the Sonoran Desert to illustrate the world's deserts.

THE FACE OF THE DESERT

In the desert, the architecture of the earth's surface can be clearly seen. Rugged mountains rise abruptly from bare flats. Dry stream beds lie deep down between cliffs of the streams' cutting. Mud floors of empty lakes are cracked by the sun.

Strangely enough, the architect and sculptor of these desert landscapes is running water. Rain comes rarely, but when it does come it falls in a violent torrent. Wild streams rush down the bare mountain slopes and bite deeply into the rock, carving it into odd forms. As they sweep away rock fragments, the streams pile up this sediment at the foot of the mountains in gently sloping alluvial fans. Then they spread out over the desert, cutting their own channels. Sometimes, when the rock beneath is soft, they carve mazes of narrow canyons and ridges known as badlands.

These streams seldom reach the sea. The flood waters pour down dry washes, ending up in closed basins. There they form temporary lakes called playas. But the waters soon seep into the parched earth and disappear, leaving a flooring of mud that bakes cement-hard under the desert sun. Because of its hardness and the salts in it, few plants grow on this dry lake flooring, though around the edges there may be a green ring of salt-bush and mesquite.

Desert badlands (below, right). Here at the foot of mountains, furrowed by ages of heavy erosion, swift-running desert floods have carved soft rock canyons and ridges.

A wind-sheared bush (below, left) was given this shape by desert winds blowing over the sheltering rock at right.

Kangaroo rat (left) leaps to escape a king snake. The snake gets moisture by eating moist-fleshed animals. Kangaroo rats, on the other hand, make moisture in their own bodies from carbohydrates present in dry seeds they eat.

Usually no more than a fifth of the desert is covered with vegetation. For the rest there are only sand and gravel and rock. Where sands are constantly wind-blown, dunes may form and move across the landscape. More common are areas where coarse bits of rock laid down by water are smoothed by wind into a desert "pavement."

Wind often blows hard across the desert, since no trees bar its way. It carries sand which blasts objects in its path, rubbing them down to smooth, wind-carved outlines. Finer particles of dust are spiralled up by the wind into thin clouds which dim the sun; these are the great dust storms.

On windless days the sun alone can trouble the desert air. Heated by the blaze of noon, the

Packrat (bottom, left) like other desert vegetarians gets ample water from prickly-pear cactus—90 percent water.

air layer closest to the ground may form a refracting layer that bends light waves from above. It can produce an inverted image of a distant object or reflect the blue ocean of sky as a view of a lake or river. That is the cause of the mirages of distant water sometimes seen shimmering in the desert heat. Here and there, though, where underground water comes to the surface, a real green oasis glistens.

ANIMALS OF THE WATERLESS WORLD

The main problem of desert animals is how to survive in a world where fresh water is rare. One might suppose that the animals of the desert are desperate for water, and weak for lack of it. On the contrary, the creatures of the desert are as healthy and contented as animals anywhere else. They are at home in their bleak environment.

Though water is the basis of life, many creatures of the desert pass their entire lives without drinking a single drop. They get it from food. In deserts you find no moist-skinned animals.

In the desert few large animals live; the giants of the American desert are the deer, the coyote, and the bobcat. Since desert country is open, it has more swift-footed, running and leaping creatures than the tangled forests. Its animals live largely by night—a silent, stealthy folk.

Having learned long generations ago to live in the desert, these animals are as healthy as any on earth. They know the burning power of the sun. Few would survive if they went out at noonday. But while the surface of the sun-baked noontime desert averages around 150°F., 18 inches down the temperature is only 60°F. So many animals pass the burning hours in cool, damp burrows underground.

All living things need water to survive. Most desert animals will drink water if they happen upon it, but many of them never do. So they find it in other forms. The herbivores or plant-eaters find moisture in desert plants. The carnivores or flesh-eaters find it in the flesh of their prey.

One of the most remarkable adjustments has been made by the tiny kangaroo rat, which not only lives without drinking but exists on a diet of dry seeds containing only 5 per cent of free water. Like other animals it manufactures water in its body by converting carbohydrates. And it conserves its small supply by every means, losing only very small amounts in its waste products and through evaporation.

Peccaries (below, centre) are wild pigs, also called javelinas. Here they dig around the roots of a prickly cholla.

Bobcat (below, right) gets both food and moisture from eating flesh, such as the ground squirrel it feeds on here.

The desert by day. At dawn, night hunters come home, and daytime animals begin to stir. At left are a spotted skunk and a gila monster (under the green collared lizard's rock). A packrat and a white-footed mouse are in burrows below. Above the sleeping skunk a chuckwalla peers forth. An antelope ground

DAY ON THE DESERT

As dawn breaks, the first creatures to rise are the birds. They cannot stand high temperature, so they feed early in the morning or late in the afternoon. During the hot hours they rest in their nests, often tucked safely among the prickly cactus spines.

Some birds will fly long distances in search of springs and pools. But most birds, like Leconte's thrasher and Gambel's quail (above), get their moisture from berries, seeds, insects, and spiders. The flesh-eating birds, like the turkey vulture, the swift road-runner, and the shrike, get moisture from their prey.

Lizards are daytime animals. Being cold-blooded, they like some sun warmth, but even the chuckwalla likes his cool rock crevice. The

squirrel nibbles cactus blossoms, a thrasher pecks in the sand beneath the cactus wren, and a jackrabbit dozes in the shade. A bullsnake slithers by, near a desert tortoise. Badger suns himself while coyote naps under a creosote bush and, underground, pocket mouse, kit fox, and kangaroo rat rest. In background,

chuckwalla is a vegetarian, fond of flowers. The collared lizard is a cannibal who eats his own kind. The horned lizard loves to lap up ants as they appear from anthills.

In methods of defence, too, the lizards differ. The gridiron-tailed lizard can run on his hind legs up to 15 miles per hour. The chuckwalla squeezes into a rocky crevice and inflates himself with air, until it is almost impossible to pull

him out. The desert iguana, if caught by the tail, simply sheds the tail and grows another one later.

Two other reptiles which like the daylight hours (though not hot sun) are the bullsnake and the desert tortoise. But few mammals are active. Even peccaries and the lively ground squirrel (seen above) avoid the hottest hours. Jackrabbits may appear in early morning, but they

135

three peccaries hunt food while a turkey vulture circles. On the sands are a desert iguana (above kit fox); long-tailed road-runner, pursuing gridiron-tailed lizard; behind them two Gambel's quail. In foreground is a horned lizard, with a round-tailed ground squirrel scampering off (right) and a shrike in the creosote bush.

too feel the heat and often seek shade later.

Noon and early afternoon are quiet hours on the desert. Coyote dozes in the shade of a creosote bush. Badger suns himself in the mouth of his burrow. Spotted skunk and gila monster find cool rock cavities. And underground burrows shelter packrat, kangaroo rat, white-footed mouse, pocket mouse, and kit fox.

Only desert plants dare face the sun. Giant saguaros here rise tree-high, with delicate yellow-green paloverde trees, flame-tipped deer-horn chollas, barrel cactus, teddy-bear cactus, and prickly pear close by. On the sandy slopes to the right are green creosote bushes and silvery, prickly bursage. All these plants have scant leaf surfaces to evaporate precious moisture.

As the day ends, and silver dusk comes on, the desert seems to come alive.

The desert by night finds the ring-tailed cat on the rock ledge (left) above the chuckwalla, sleeping in his crevice. Packrat busily adds litter to cover his nest, while below sleeps antelope ground squirrel. Horned owl glides toward spotted skunk (ready to strike with his powerful scent) and diamondback rattlesnake.

NIGHT ON THE DESERT

Beneath the desert stars, the unending battles of the hunters and the hunted go on. Now, snug in their homes, the creatures of the day lie sleeping —chuckwalla, ground squirrel, tortoise, iguana, and horned lizard lightly covered with sand. Bullsnake sleeps in some rodent's home—with the rodent inside him.

Nearly every creature represents a meal for some other larger than itself. The plant-eating rodents, for example, are food for mammals, reptiles, and birds. Packrat is the favourite of handsome ring-tailed cat. White-footed mouse, kangaroo rat, and pocket mouse are in great demand. White-footed mouse likes to vary its vegetable diet with insects and spiders; kangaroo rat and pocket mouse collect seeds and hoard them in

137

FOLD OUT—DO NOT TEAR

Bullsnake and desert tortoise sleep in underground burrows. Coyote pursues jackrabbit in background. In foreground, timid white-footed mouse and kangaroo rat (seen from rear) venture out for food. Gila monster waits under a creosote bush; sidewinder swings himself along in sidewise loops, just above the

their burrows. If kangaroo rat is attacked, he can leap high in the air, and he kicks sand into the eyes of the hunter.

Jackrabbit is hunted, too; but he can run 45 miles an hour, leap 15 feet. Skunk is both hunted and hunter, eating cactus fruits, insects, mice, and baby rabbits. When pursued he can spray his powerful oil or stand on his hands to confuse hunters. Horned owl especially likes skunk meat.

Gila monster, a rare poisonous reptile, slowly crawls about hunting squirrel, rabbits, and quail eggs. More dangerous and bolder are rattlesnake and sidewinder.

Among larger mammals, ring-tailed cat stays on the rocky slopes, hunting packrats. Shy and dainty kit fox prefers kangaroo rats. Few hunters can catch the swift kit fox, but one of the few is bobcat, sly and fierce. It dwells in rugged canyons

burrow of sleeping iguana. Kit fox eyes a tasty pocket mouse while bobcat eyes kit fox. Badger digs hopefully into a burrow at the foot of a night-blooming cereus. In the sky (centre) bats circle, hunting moths and other insects. In background (to left of flying bat) are yucca blossoms, called "the Lord's candles."

and ledge country by day, coming down only at night to prowl the flats.

Another fearless hunter is badger, who lives boldly in open places where he can dig open the homes of rodents.

Monarch of the flats and best-known of desert animals is the handsome, lean coyote, whose lonely howls resound at dusk across the sands. He is a good hunter and digger, but will also eat·

cactus or mesquite beans, or another animal's kill.

All night the desert is the scene of small, swift battles for life. But as the stars fade, the animals retire. One of the last to go is leather-winged bat, who has spent the dark hours fluttering about in pursuit of moths and other insects. Before he crawls into his rock crevice, birds of the day are on the wing again.

WHEN THE RAINS COME

In time, rains do come to the desert. In winter, they may come in on the westerly winds; in summer, there are local thunderstorms to drench the earth now and then.

Thunderstorms, like the one here, start when warm, moist air blows into an area where heat has made the air rise, leaving pressure near the ground very low. The moist air, rising too, reaches cooler heights, and its water vapour condenses there into rain or even frozen hail. This falls in great sheets, with lightning and thunder.

When this torrent of water strikes the desert, the hard-baked surface sheds the water as a paved road would. The water quickly finds its way into dry channels or washes, and rushes furiously down them, tearing at loose shrubs, soil, and rock. Soon, loaded with mud and debris, the flash flood is pouring through canyons in destructive fury.

But the rain soon stops. The flow from upstream dies away, and the flood loses its force. The soil has now lost its hard surface; it soaks up moisture thirstily. Some water finds its way to a playa and spreads out as a short-lived lake. A few days later only mud remains, cracking under the desert sun.

A pillar of rain slants down from a thunderhead in the distance, bringing a deluge like the one above. The clear area, centre, may get no rain.

140

A summer thunderstorm lashes this Arizona desert with wind, water, and hail. Such downpours come mainly in summer, when moist air comes in on seasonal winds from the Gulf of Mexico. Heating of the land in southern Arizona causes low-pressure centres. Here warm, moist air spirals upward, creating thunderheads which explode with heavy rains.

A flash flood rushes down the channel of a desert slope in a sudden wild torrent.

A day later the same wash channel is dry again except for scattered muddy patches, which sun will soon bake dry.

Saguaro blossoms (above). The saguaro is a giant cactus, often tree-high. During May its spiny stalks are capped with delicate, waxy blossoms—state flower of Arizona.

Hedgehog cactus blossoms (above). This cactus is a squat, foot-high, branched variety. Its blooms brighten rocky desert ledges and are followed by juicy, edible fruit.

Mariposa lilies are among the loveliest of Southwestern flowers. Bulbs live through dry periods, while the plant dies back, to bloom again after rain.

THE DESERT BLOSSOMS

Desert rains do not always vanish without a trace. The year-round desert plants have ways of using those sudden downpours. Many cacti have spreading root systems that can absorb a lot of water in a single rainstorm, and in their thick stems they can store that moisture for dry months to come.

Most plants give off moisture constantly from their leaf surfaces. Desert plants, which cannot afford to do this, have reduced leaf surfaces. Cacti leaves are sharp needles. Other plants, like the paloverde, have tiny leaves. Still others, like the ocotillo, shed all their leaves during long dry spells. The brittle bush lets whole branches die back, keeping its roots alive. Thus permanent plant inhabitants withstand the desert's harshness and the fickleness of rain.

But the desert has equally remarkable plants which once or twice a year brighten the desert scene. These are the flowering annuals. After

Barrel cactus blossoms (left). The tough, springy spines were used by Indians for fishhooks. Blossoms appear on the bristly stem in March or April.

Spring blooms on the desert after rain. In dry season, seeds of flowering annuals lie dormant. Rain makes them swiftly flower. Here we see desert dandelions, white evening primroses, and purple sand verbena.

rain breaks a dry spell, they burst into bloom, carpeting the once-bleak desert valleys with varied colours. During the dry months the seeds have slept. Now, awakened by the freshening rain, they germinate, flower, and bear seeds—all in a swift, bright, astonishingly brief six or eight weeks. Among all the manifestations of nature this remains one of the most magnificent.

Caribou file across a frozen lake. Beyond, the Canadian tundra stretches emptily northward.

PART X

THE ARCTIC BARRENS

THE TUNDRA AND ITS SETTING

FAR IN THE north, where the last stunted trees bow to the power of icy winds, the land opens out into a bleak and barren plain. This is the tundra—the frozen prairie, the arctic wilderness which rings the Northern Hemisphere—and the Northern only—below the polar sea.

The arctic (northern) and antarctic (southern) regions differ in important ways. The South Pole is on a continent—high, savagely cold, windy—with the Antarctic Ocean around it. Much is unexplored. Within the Antarctic Circle no human beings live permanently, and no land animals larger than insects.

By contrast the Arctic is a much milder and friendlier region. The North Pole is situated in a sea surrounded by the land of the tundra. Within the Arctic Circle there are cities and towns; tall forests flourish and animal life abounds. In summer most of the land enjoys mild and even warm weather. Snow melts, plants bloom, birds flock from the south. Even the arctic sea, kept mild by shifting currents from the south, never freezes solid. Its ice floes are 10 to 100 feet thick, but they keep circling the pole in slow motion.

In the polar region proper, snow and ice never vanish. But in the circle of the tundra, for two or three months of the year the land turns green.

This tundra is an enormous reach of bleak, treeless plain which circles the globe between the polar sea and the tree line. It includes most of northern

Tundra circles Arctic Ocean (map at right) in treeless band shown here by black line.

Canada, Siberia, Russia, the Scandinavian countries, parts of Alaska, and some islands. It exists only in the north. There is no tundra in the Antarctic.

By contrast again with the wild Antarctic, the arctic tundra is one of the least stormy regions on earth. During the winter it is overhung with a semi-permanent high-pressure air mass of still, dry air. Daily variations in temperature are slight, because in winter there is so little sunlight, and in summer the sunlight is almost constant. The tundra has, therefore, few of the air movements that lead to changes in weather. Strong winds are rare; the average for the Canadian tundra is 6 miles per hour. What storms there are come principally in spring and fall, when temperature changes are more pronounced.

As to scenery, the arctic tundra has occasional mountains and rivers, as in Siberia. In Canada there are bleak fields of frost-shattered rock and gravel. But most of the tundra rolls away flat and featureless save for innumerable lakes and ponds. The flatness is the result of long erosion and the 2-mile-thick ice sheet which scoured away the hills and ridges in the glacial Pleistocene.

The special feature of the tundra is permafrost. This is the name geologists give to the ice in permanently frozen ground. The southern edges of the permafrost mark the boundary of the arctic.

Stunted birches on Sweden's alpine tundra. This is thinly forested wasteland with higher altitude than arctic tundra farther north.

The tree line—where the forests of the north end and the arctic plain begins.

Only the topmost inches of the tundra thaw each summer, permitting plants to grow. The thaw does not go deep enough for real tree roots to grow. Nor does it go deep enough to permit much water to drain off to rivers and the sea. Most of the rain and snow that fall is trapped in the lakes and ponds which form in every small hollow and cover half the tundra surface.

Our north polar cap, you will remember, shrinks a little each year. Each summer its southern rim is a little farther north than it was the summer before. In the same way the southern edges of the permafrost move north a few hundred feet each year. If all the permafrost some day melts, if the water runs off into the sea, and if rains on the tundra are no heavier than they are now (about 11 inches a year), then the tundra will become the greatest desert on earth.

THE ARCTIC YEAR

For nine months of the year, winter holds the heart of the tundra. Day by day, from late June onward, the sun's path moves nearer the horizon, and the nights grow ever longer. By September, lakes and ponds vanish under sheaths of ice. Flowing waters are stilled. The first snows come early and cover the barrens with a light coating.

A **winding river** meanders in broad curves across the tundra's level plain, by its many lakes. The plains pictured here, the Canadian barrens, are green with short-lived summer plants.

The barren ground of the tundra is grooved by glaciers, pocked with ponds.

North of the Arctic Circle the sun drops below the horizon in early December. Then the great cold settles in. In winter the tundra is colder than the ice-packed arctic sea, colder than the North Pole itself. For ocean currents tend to warm the polar area, while the more southerly tundra is kept cold by a shield of ice and snow.

The coldest temperature ever noted in the polar ice pack was −62°F., but in the Canadian tundra −82°F. was once registered, and the Siberian tundra holds the world's official record of −93.6°F.

In the long winter night the skies shimmer and glow with the ghostly lights of the aurora borealis. Not until mid-January does the sun return each day, and then it only arches briefly above the horizon. There are still long months of cold ahead for man and beast.

Toward the end of May, when the sun once more completes its circle above the horizon day and night, the snows melt and the ice on rivers and lakes breaks up noisily, casting strangely shaped blocks up on the muddy shores. But this early spring is a dreary time, sodden with melt waters, shrouded with low clouds and curtains of mist.

In the whole winter the average snowfall will only equal 2 inches of rain, but all the world is white. On days of overcast, the white land and white sky blend into an endless, soul-wearying emptiness.

Spring torrents, swollen with the run-off water of melting snow, rush wildly across the tundra during break-up, emptying into the sea or larger lakes. Because they have no permanent water source, these streams disappear in the summer.

148

Arctic Ocean ice floes here grind against a headland 1,000 feet high. This picture was taken in August, when hardy grasses lent a tinge of green to the brown, nearly bare, sun-warmed heights.

From May to July there is no darkness. On quiet afternoons great cumulus clouds mass overhead, towering above the flat earth. At night, when the rose-pink sun dips for a little while beneath the horizon, the sky remains alive with light.

It is in the middle of June that the arctic plants appear in a carpet of colour. Swiftly, miraculously then, warmed by the constant sunlight, come the flowers—forget-me-nots, lupines, poppies. The muddy shores of the lakes and streams become bright with gold and green, jewelled with brilliant bits of colour. Birds arrive from the south, and loud insect noises fill the air.

In this brief interlude of summer the tundra comes fully alive. Hundreds of species of arctic plants spread across the bogs and marshes, and many birds and animals come to nibble at them. But the greens soon turn to red and yellow. The animals and birds soon head south again, but for a hardy few. For the first bleak breath of autumn comes out of the north before August ends. By September the lonely land again is white, and winter has returned.

The spring tundra, seen here in the warm light of a June morning, is bright with colour. Orange and coral-coloured lichens grow on the frost-cracked boulders. Last year's dry grass gleams golden; melt water on a thawing lake reflects the pale blue sky; and a chalk-white caribou skull lies bleaching under the sun.

Patterned earth is a decorative land form in Alaska and other tundra areas. These geometric forms are created by action of ground frost and are common on tundras. Shown here in mid-July, they are bright with summer vegetation and checkered with patches of standing water.

FEATURES OF THE EARTH

On the tundra there are few great heights or depths, no mountains being uplifted, no valleys carved. For untold years the permafrost has preserved the tundra from erosion. But the top few inches of the surface soil thaw each year, and there is constant activity in those surface inches.

"Patterned ground" is one of the features of the tundra which result from the repeated freezing and thawing of the soil. When water freezes, it expands; and when it thaws, it contracts. So there is constant working of the wet soil through the year. Patches of fine silt and clay hold more moisture than coarse, gravelly soils. When the ground freezes, therefore, the finer materials, containing more water, expand more and thrust the gravel and stones outward in all directions.

A layer of ground ice 2 feet thick lies sandwiched between a cover of grassy vegetation and a base of silty clay. This layer may have formed when a pond froze and was buried.

A giant frost heave called a pingo rises 330 feet from the floor of an old tundra lake bed. Its dark outer covering of earth is cloaked with lichens and other vegetation, but its core is ice.

This process is repeated season after season, resulting in a sorting out of the soils. The stones are pushed to the rim of circular patterns ranging from a few inches to 30 feet in diameter. This is the most generally accepted explanation for patterned ground—certainly one of the odd and interesting sights of northern lands.

Other factors are at work in the tundra too, so these patterns vary. Sometimes the shrinking action of great cold causes the soil to draw in, leaving grooves instead of stone rows between patterns. Often the patterns are polygons—many-sided shapes—instead of circles. Sometimes on gentle slopes the soil creeps downhill over the permafrost, stretching the patterns into stripes.

Bedrock is sometimes shattered by frost, and

151

huge slabs have even been stood up on end. Or frost may heave up small columns of soil, to be capped in summer with grasses.

Most spectacular of all are the giant volcano-like mounds called pingoes. These are huge frost-heaves, pushed up by the tremendous pressures when layers of unfrozen material are squeezed between a frozen top layer and the permafrost.

THE FLOWERING TUNDRA

The tundra, surprisingly, is carpeted with plants almost everywhere. Even at the top of Greenland, 400 miles from the pole, dozens of varieties of ferns spring up, and flowering plants bloom each spring. The Canadian tundra has countless spe-

Marsh fleabane (above) is a flowering tundra plant able to grow only in marshy bogs of the southern arctic regions.

Bearberry leaves (below) are bright against green of alpine cranberry. Berry plants grow in thick mats in dry, poor soil.

Arctic cotton grass produces these silky white balls each summer. They rise on slender, reedlike stems from shallow fresh-water pools to present a rich, tropical appearance against surrounding frost-worn, bleak rocks.

Small grass-covered hummocks of frozen earth are often found in marshes which are thick with plants. They are called "têtes de femmes," or ladies' heads, and are probably formed by upheavals due to frost. Protected from the sun by little "hats" of grass, they are slow to thaw.

Lichens are slow-growing, primitive plants, which do very well in the drier parts of the frozen earth. They are the most important food plants of the foraging caribou. When these coral-like lichens are eaten away, the herds must move to new pastures.

A **lichen ring** spreads over the rock on which it grows. Each year the outer edges awaken and spread new growth across the rock. Meanwhile the centre slowly dies and falls away.

White heather bells give a touch of life and colour to the bleak heath for a few weeks in spring. Heather grows in low places where snow gives it protective cover in winter.

cies, from primitive mosses and lichens to ground birch, willow, flowering shrubs, and heather.

Like desert plants, the plants of the tundra must be especially equipped for life in a harsh climate. For nine months of the year arctic waters are locked in ice. The soil is acid, badly drained, and cold. Roots cannot poke down deeply into it. The plants are generally small and compact, with shallow, spreading root systems and small, tough leaves. Many do not depend on seeds, but reproduce by budding. When perpetual daylight comes, tundra plants awake and swiftly bloom.

Near the pole, where only simple forms of life can grow, the lichens live. These flat, rootless plants grow everywhere on earth, but seem especially well suited to the arctic because they can withstand dry cold and can live on bare rock. Simple, primitive, lichens are usually the first plants to appear on barren ground. As they spread they prepare the land for higher forms.

How can the lichens grow on rock? They are made up of two distinct organisms, working together. One is a fungus (which must live on other living or once-live matter); the other is an alga, seaweed-like. The fungus produces acids that eat away the rock, supplying necessary minerals to the alga. In return the alga supplies the organic (live) matter on which the fungus lives.

To lichens the tundra owes much of its continuous plant cover, and caribou much of their food.

Fireweed (or broad-leaved willow herb) is the largest, showiest arctic flower, found in nearly all the arctic lands of the world. It grows in large patches on dry sand and gravel.

Orange lichen is the brightest of arctic lichens. It grows mostly on rocks where owls and hawks perch. The nitrogen-rich droppings left by the birds form valuable fertiliser.

WANDERERS IN A WIDE LAND

Largest of all the herd animals of the tundra is the musk ox. There are only a few hundred left on the mainland of North America, none at all in

A black filigree effect is created by this lichen growing on a pink boulder. The photo was made just after sundown.

Winter (to left) and summer (to right) on the tundra find the mighty musk ox, arctic hares in their snow-white winter coats, and a white-furred arctic fox. Next are some of the tundra birds (from left), including willow ptarmigans (male, left, and female), rock ptarmigan (foreground), and, flying low in the

Musk oxen of Cornwallis Island here feed on purple saxifrage, an herb which grows on moist rocks in the far north.

Europe and Asia. Perhaps 35,000 live on Greenland and some of the arctic islands. Men have tried to domesticate them, because their meat is good to eat. But so far they have failed. Eskimos and Indians hunt them, though, and man is largely responsible for the dwindling numbers.

The musk ox is well equipped for life on the tundra. His thick coat defends him against the cold of winter as well as the ferocious flies of summer. To meet attacks of fierce arctic wolves he has heavy horns, surprising agility, and group defence. When attacked, the oxen stand shoulder to shoulder in a protective line to defend themselves and the young of the herd.

Simple herbs satisfy the musk oxen, and they find food even under the snow. They do not often need to move to fresh pastures. They may spend their whole lives within a hundred-mile radius.

background, a snowy owl. In the centre sits a red fox, now in his summer coat of brown. Rippling the pond, at right, is a globe-trotting northern phalarope. On the near shore stand a semipalmated plover and a golden plover. Left of caribou skull are snow buntings. Background, upper right, distant caribou head north.

Much more numerous are the caribou, wild cousins of the domesticated European reindeer. The caribou population of the Canadian tundra is about 75,000, constantly on the move.

Each spring before the surface snow melts, the caribou come out of the forests where they have wintered, and head across the tundra. Cows and yearlings lead the long, straggling ranks. Bulls lag several days behind. Caribou follow old migration trails. Seldom do they wander from their route even to escape wolves—or summer plagues of flies.

Northward, always northward, they move across the greening tundra, across rivers and lakes, sometimes to the polar sea. The cows stop at last and drop their calves. In about two weeks the new calves have strength to travel. Then the herd turns about.

Now, with cows and calves trailing after the bulls, all start slowly back toward the forests to the south. Footsore from their long journey, they walk slowly, with an ambling gait, cropping the summer lichens, mosses, and grasses. Their coats are thin and flybitten, for this is the shedding season. Some caribou are driven to madness by the numberless needles of the warble flies, which lay their eggs in the hides of the caribou.

Late in the summer the cows and bulls mingle and travel for a time in a mixed herd, back to their winter home in the woods.

The mightiest animal of the tundra, the barren-ground grizzly, stalks the plains alone. A vegetarian at heart, eating masu root, licorice root, and berries, he robs the ground squirrels' stores of roots when he can. In hard times he will even eat grass.

Summary (to left) **and fall** (to right) **on the tundra** find a whistling swan· (far left), well-fed-looking ground squirrels, and a lanky sandhill crane enjoying the mild season. Two ducks swimming at left, foreground, are old squaws; a red-breasted merganser is following close behind. As the colder days of fall come on (centre

Some other animals of the tundra prefer herd life, though. In addition to the musk oxen and caribou, there are arctic hares which scamper across the rocky soil. On the southern tundra hares change colour in the spring. As the snow melts they and the snowy ptarmigans and arctic foxes all discard their bright white coats for more ground-coloured ones. But far north, where snow is on the ground most of the year, the hares keep their white coats all year around. They are so skilful at finding food that they often reach a weight of 14 pounds.

Birds, too, travel in flocks in the arctic, as they do elsewhere. The rock ptarmigans or arctic grouse huddle through the winter, in their white feathers, in any scant shrubbery they can find. They come out onto the open land in the spring. Then, protected by ground-brown feathers, they

·nest on the bare ground, unseen for the most part by circling hawks and prowling foxes. But in case of danger, the males stand guard over the females on the nests, strutting with fierce-looking pride.

Soon after the ptarmigans move out into the open, the true migrants arrive. Many have come from warm lands far away. Among these is the northern phalarope, who has flown thousands of miles from the South Atlantic to nest and rear young beside the tundra lakes.

Snow buntings flutter like white flower petals across the barrens, and the shores of ponds and rivers are bright with plovers, standing at attention in their golden feather finery.

Overhead wheel the long-tailed jaegers, those patient hunters, enemy of gull and tern.

By July the waters ripple in the wake of many ducks. From every lake and riverbank resound

of picture) the barren-ground caribou, already footsore and weary, head south for the approaching winter. Three lesser Canada geese have alighted on the rocky ground here (foreground) for a rest before continuing their own long journey south. Soon snow will fall, and the tundra will sleep in the loneliness of arctic night.

the *Woo-hoo Woo-hoo Woo-hoo* of the whistling swan, and the deep, rolling, trumpet-like *Krooo* of the sandhill crane.

Canada geese in their sharp V-formations fly northward and return south in the fall. The skies echo with their lonely, honking cries.

As autumn colours the arctic plains with red and gold, the lemmings sense the approach of winter and expand their straw-lined burrows. These plump little rodents are the favourite food of foxes, weasels, hawks, and owls. But sometimes their numbers grow so that there is not food enough in the area for them. Then they migrate as a group. Away they go, stopping for nothing—not even rushing water or deep fjords. Sometimes whole bands are drowned in one of these attempted crossings.

Legends say the lemmings commit mass sui-cide. They may die in bands, but it is not suicide.

After a lemming migration, the arctic foxes have some slim hunting seasons until the lemming population builds up again.

Gradually as the days of autumn fade, the sounds and movements of the summer die away with the light of the sun. The last stragglers of the caribou disappear toward the south. The last birds wing southward overhead. The arctic fox and arctic hare all but disappear from view in their coats of winter white.

Silence descends upon the barren grounds, and hunger for the animals who stay. It is small wonder that the arctic wolf needs to be fiercer than his woodland cousins, and that the arctic fox cunningly stores away food. For as snowflakes fall over frozen plants, and the tundra sleeps in twilight, the desperate winter begins.

PART XI

THE RAIN FOREST

EVER GREEN, EVER GROWING

Millions of years ago, before the ice ages, the green rain forests spread out from the equator two thirds of the way to the poles. With the approach of the ice, they shrank southward. Behind them hardier conifers and deciduous (leaf-shedding) trees sprang up. But even today, evergreen rain forests still blanket millions of square miles of moist lowlands along the equator—more than a tenth of the planet's land surface and nearly half of the forest areas.

In a true rain forest the spreading canopy of interwoven treetops filters the sun's rays. On the dim forest floor, little can grow but a few shrubs and saplings. In the dark, roomy aisles between the straight tree trunks the ground is quite open, with only a thin carpet of the leaves that flutter down all year around. Only where the grand trees have been cut can the tangle of undergrowth, creepers, and vines called the "bush" spring up.

Most rain forest plants are woody and treelike. "Violets" grow bigger than our apple trees. "Myrtles" have woody stems as thick as a man's thigh. "Roses" tower 150 feet high. These are members of the same families we know; but in cool climates they are smaller.

The rain forest is taller, generally, than forests of temperate zones. Trees average 110 to 120 feet; some reach 200 feet. Most leaves are large, leathery, and dark green. Among the trees dangle sinewy lianas and other climbing plants, sometimes tightly drawn, sometimes in loops like tinsel on a Christmas tree.

Near the equator there are two rainy seasons a year. Even in "dry" seasons there may be 3 to 4 inches of rain a month. In a year the average is 150 inches.

During rainy seasons, cloudbursts pour down as much as 30 inches of water in 30 days. The forest drips almost continuously, even under fair skies. By day the wind and sun cannot reach through to the ground to carry off the moisture; even by night the damp heat is imprisoned there. New leaves spring out to cover every chink that may appear in the cover.

From season to season, there is little change in the rain forest. But it is always richer in the variety of its plant and animal life than any other area on earth, save perhaps the sea. Woods in the temperate zone may have a few dozen varieties of trees at most. A square mile of rain forest has 200 or 300, counting only trees with trunks more than a foot in diameter. Smaller trees are just as varied. And so are the animals that live at every level, from floor to sunlit roof.

A **bromeliad** (left), an air plant of the rain forest, clings to a branch over a stream.

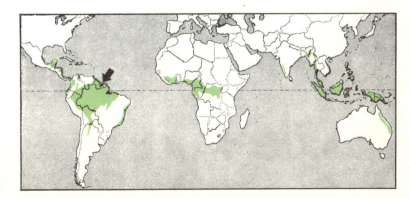

The rain forests (green areas) form a girdle around the equator. They cover more than one-tenth of the earth's land surface. Arrow indicates rain forest described here.

TYPES OF FORESTS

From the air the forest appears as an unending ocean of treetops, as much alike as the ocean's waves. But on the ground we find a bewildering variety of plants and animals.

There are choked creeks running through the twilit forests, with the land rolling gently between them. Small plateaux of bare sand or rock here and there break the growth. Swamps and bogs with strange twisted trees arch above them. There are slow rivers walled with solid masses of plants.

Botanists find rain-forest plants in such variety that they divide up the region for study. They speak of "dry rain forests" on sandy hills; "swamp forests" in flooded vales; "montane rain forests" on foggy mountain slopes; and "gallery forests" by the shores of streams that flow through dry grassy lands.

The completely non-seasonal rain forest called "climax" is found only in

A small savannah, or grassy plain (above), breaks the forest pattern. Behind the sand and scrub a gallery forest looms high in the distance. Its treetops are bedecked thickly with flowers.

A palm bog (left) has formed with dense, thin-stemmed undergrowth. Soaked earth and stagnant water have stunted trees.

sheltered, well-drained lowlands where at least 4 inches of rain fall in every month. Where the rain sometimes is a bit less, tree leaves fall, and blossoming is not as even the year around; these are called "evergreen seasonal rain forests." And confusingly, many of these types may be crowded together within a single square mile!

There is variety enough on any one spot in the rain forest. From the ground towers a many-storied mansion of trees. In the lower story are sparse young trees up to 60 feet tall, struggling for life in the gloom. From 60 to 120 feet rise taller, sturdier trees whose round, branched crowns form the forest canopy. Then, 120 to 200 feet or more from the ground tower the giants. Their crowns have burst through the canopy into the sunny upper air, like tropic islands above a green sea. Each layer of that sea receives a different amount of sunlight, and, like the layers of ocean reaching down into gloom, has its own plant and animal life.

Above the canopy, the mists of morning curl upward as the rising sun's heat warms the foliage. Here, 125 feet above the ground, the mists will soon vanish as the sun rises. But under the roof of trees the shadowed forest lies steeped in moisture, dawn to dusk.

THE FOREST FLOOR

At the foot of the great trees is a sunless world where the life of the forest has its beginnings and endings.

Trees begin sometimes in a process known as cauliflowering, or stem flowering. They produce flowers on their main trunks and branches, near the ground. There crawling and low-flying insects carry pollen from blossom to blossom. Seeds develop from the flowers. And from the seeds come tiny saplings, reaching upward to the half-light.

The new trees rise out of the graveyards of the old. Season after season, leaves fall to the forest floor, there to nourish saplings. Occasionally a giant, too, dies and falls—if there is room to fall. But the litter on the forest floor is thin, because agents of destruction work rapidly upon it—water, fungi, bacteria, worms, and insects. As the litter decays, the feeding roots of the forest consume it. Thus most of the forest's richness is always locked up in the form of living vegetation.

Toadstools rise up through the

A leaning dome (below) 2 inches high is raised by gill fungus **Lepiota.** This mushroom, like a little monument raised by forest elves, is a common ornament of the tropical forest.

A tree seed (left), almost entirely fluff, lies among leaves on forest floor. The slightest breeze may carry it to a locality where it can start growing.

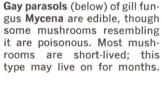

thick carpet of rain-moist leaves.

CREATURES OF THE SHADE

Among bright blossoms and decaying leaves on the forest floor live the creatures of the shade (pages 166-167). At dawn or dusk one hears their voices, glimpses flickering shapes. Here are opossums, an ancient mammal; the philander, quica, and timid marmosa. Here are anteaters, ancient too; and giant armadillo, paca, and the agouti. Largest are the shy tapir, long-nosed cousin of the rhinoceros, and the puma and the jaguar. Smaller hunters are two cats which like the jaguar climb trees—the margay and the bird-eating yaguarundi; and a ferocious 4-foot weasel, the tayra.

Older even than the forest are turtles, tortoises, toads, lizards, and some of the snakes—the 25-foot anaconda of forest waters, the boa constrictor, and the deadly bushmaster and the fer de lance. Birds, too, flourish here, many solemnly dressed for life in the shadows, and insects as numberless as the leaves!

Gay parasols (below) of gill fungus **Mycena** are edible, though some mushrooms resembling it are poisonous. Most mushrooms are short-lived; this type may live on for months.

Spiny bush grapes (right) too, are fruits of the rain forest. The low-growing blossoms attract low-flying and crawling insects.

165

Creatures of the Shade. Here are some of the tropical rain forest's numberless inhabitants. At left, coming out of the pool, is a giant otter with a fish in its mouth. It faces a matamata turtle, an anaconda, and—above—a Guiana partridge. To the otter's right a crab-eating raccoon hunts his dinner. Near his tail is a Surinam toad, and beyond, a water opossum rests by the water. The fancy bird at the base of the tree is a Cayenne guan. To its right is a tapir. Above it, to the left, are a sun bittern and (top) a scarlet cock of the rock. On the tree, left, is a common opossum. Two bluish curassows are on the thick vine, upper left centre, and to their right, lower, a philander opossum and a quica crawl down the tree. At the base of this tree is a boa constrictor facing a paca (a large rodent), behind which is another tropical rodent. A tegu lizard and a tiny marmosa are on the long liana near the paca. Beyond the lizard are a

yaguarundi, two greyish peccaries, and (far back) a jaguar. To the right of the peccaries are a pair of red brocket deer and a giant anteater. Flying above these is a tinamou. The snakes to the right of the stump are a cribo snake and a yellow-lipped tree snake. To the left of the stump is a wood rail; to the right, a greenish marbled tree lizard is climbing up the stump toward the gecko near the top. Near the base of the giant tree in the right background a puma prowls. Nearer us are a bush dog, a giant armadillo, and a deadly fer de lance. Farther to the right, beneath the tree stump, a fearsome bushmaster lurks. To its right is the blue jungle runner, facing a bush spider. Two pigeons perch on top of the stump; a trumpeter is halfway down. A tayra (a jungle weasel) seems about to climb the stump. From lower right corner to rear, we see a bush tortoise, a liana snake (to right of stump), an agouti, and a spotted margay.

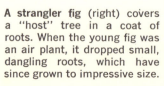

Stilt roots (left) raise this bog palm above high-water level.

A strangler fig (right) covers a "host" tree in a coat of roots. When the young fig was an air plant, it dropped small, dangling roots, which have since grown to impressive size.

An air plant (above) dangles its roots down into the water of a gallery creek for nourishment. From frail roots like these the great strangler fig on page 168 has developed.

Buttress roots (left) of an Andira tree make a huge pedestal measuring 80 feet across and 12 feet high. By contrast, the underground root system is astonishingly shallow.

THE FOREST'S FOUNDATIONS

The trees of the forest rise straight and tall, without the clutter of twigs and branches that we are used to seeing in northern woods. But the bases of these great rain-forest trees are often strangely ornamented.

Many of the smaller trees have stilt roots like those in the picture on the opposite page. They come out from the trunk as much as 10 feet above the ground, turn downward, and reach down into the soil, there to branch out in numerous rootlets. In flood forests and swamps they hold the base of the trunk above the high-water mark. Why they occur in drier areas, where there are no rising waters to touch the base of the tree, is a mystery.

Far commoner are the buttress roots of forest giants. Surrounding the trunk just above ground level, they grow on the top of shallow roots and sometimes spread out 40 feet from the tree. It may be that such roots help the trees to stand, since even giants in the tropics have very shallow roots, which storms may wrench loose from the ground, or which flowing water may undermine.

Buttresses grow in many fantastic forms. Some slope gently to the ground, while others climb sharply up into the lower leaves. Some have knife-sharp edges. Others curve like snakes. And some arch above the ground with a clear space underneath, like the flying buttresses of Gothic cathedrals. But even these stout buttresses do not keep the giants standing forever. There comes a time when water undermines the shallow roots in the thin soil, or sudden gales rock the leafy treetops, and down comes the tree, carrying smaller trees with it.

169

High up in the rain forest: Lower left corner, owl monkeys, near red-breasted motmot. Higher, an oropendula (yellowish), red chatterer, and macaws. Under macaws, two white-faced sakis; below them, kinkajous. In tree fork, top centre, a tamandua, with toucanet above, parrots and macaw to right. About tree fork, centre, red-backed sakis. A ho-ko-bee lizard on tree trunk, lower left centre; still lower, on other trunk, a tree lizard; to right, parakeet (green) snake, black Midas marmoset, and blue cotinga, with sulphur-throated toucan and toucanet above. On diagonal tree trunk, an iguana (large green reptile); at fork, a coati, and farther out on his branch a green boa, two-toed sloth, and three-toed sloth. Lower right, crested flycatcher (under two-toed sloth) and rainbow boa. Spider monkeys, right, near the greyish coendou (upper right, on tree) and tawny, spotted ocelot (upper right corner).

ACROBATS OF THE CANOPY

In the rain forest, especially of South America, live the greatest acrobats on earth. In the Old World not even monkeys can hang by their tails; but here the coonlike kinkajou, a porcupine, and two tree-dwelling anteaters can.

American monkeys, called ceboids, include marmosets, owl monkeys, sakis, spider monkeys, squirrel monkeys, howlers, and others. Among them the star is the skinny, intelligent spider monkey. Hanging head down from a climbing liana, he can launch himself 50 feet and lightly catch a bough on which he has spied a shining berry. No owl monkey or saki can do that, for their arms are shorter and their tails less skilled. The marmosets, smallest of monkeys, travel in noisy gangs. They leap well, but they land against a tree trunk, with arms and legs outspread.

Many hunters walk among the branches. These include the kinkajou, cousin to the raccoon, and the coati, who often goes down to the ground on fishing trips. Two anteaters, the golden-brown tamandua and the silky anteater, live here too. And there is a climbing cat, the dainty ocelot.

All these animals hunt the plant-eaters, among them the coendou, a porcupine; frolicsome squirrels like the small *Sciurillus;* and the two- and three-toed sloths. Slow and dull of eye, ear, and wit, the sloths hang upside down by powerful, clawed hands. Slowly they move among the branches, munching leaves. They cannot fight or flee from enemies like the eagle and jaguar, but

The roof of the forest is seen here from the crown of one of the giant trees called emergents. Here the roof-top rolls away like a sea of green, foam-flecked with flowers. In the distance another giant emergent tree has broken through the canopy. It towers above its neighbours and sprawls out under the sun. The sprays of yellow blossoms are on **Vochysia** trees. Around the lookout in the foreground are delicate, purple-hearted white trumpets and fragrant basket lianas. The large, rounded, deep-green leaves in the right foreground are those of an enormous air plant.

the green, mossy alga that grows on their long fur camouflages them among the leaves.

Even reptiles of the canopy are graceful and daring. The tiny, chameleon-like ho-ko-bee lizard can leap up and land on the under side of a branch far above, clinging with adhesive pads on his feet. The iguana can plunge 80 feet into a pool. The green tree boa and the parakeet snake pursue prey to the ends of the tiniest twigs.

All through the canopy, also, dart bright-coloured, noisy birds that seldom venture into the shadows below or the eagle-haunted upper air.

172

THE HANGING GARDENS

On top of the forest canopy with its shadowy arches stretch the roof gardens of the forest. Here warm light bathes rolling carpets of leaves. In this lovely parkland the greenery is brightened all year round by flowers whose perfumes drift constantly in the softly moving air.

Not all the blossoms in these hidden gardens spring from the trees themselves. Many come from plants reaching upward toward the light.

One such group are the lianas, climbing plants.

173

A liana (above), a climbing vine, dangles here in knots and loose spirals. Climbing plants like this monkey ladder often pull themselves up into saplings and, as these grow tall, ride up with them to the heights.

They are similar to ivy, clematis, woodbine, and other climbers of temperate woodlands. But here they grow to astonishing size. With woody stems as much as 2 feet thick and 500 feet long, they compete even with trees for space and light.

Their fantastic forms loop and spiral through the forest. On high they braid their stems from branch to branch, from one tree's crown to the next, filling every empty leaf space in the canopy. They weave the forest roof so tightly that a tree cut through at the base may lack space to fall.

Even stranger than the lianas are the epiphytes, or the air plants. This large group includes orchids, cacti, aroids, bromeliads. They flower high in the trees without benefit of soil. There are also non-flowering lichens and mosses.

The air plants attach themselves to crannies in the branches of trees and lianas. Usually they put forth a fine meshwork of roots. These collect dust and plant debris, and in time create a soil of their own. Often the roots also harbour ants, which help build up the soil by their wastes and dead bodies.

Water is scarce for the air plants, so they are adapted, like desert plants, to last through dry periods. When they do get water, they absorb it very quickly and conserve it carefully.

Some send dangling roots down through the canopy until they can take nourishment from the earth itself. Then they may grow into large and burdensome trees on top of the trees from which they started life. A few strangle their supporting

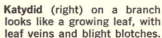

Katydid (right) on a branch looks like a growing leaf, with leaf veins and blight blotches.

Liana flower (left) hanging below the canopy is more easily reached by butterflies and bees. Many rain-forest trees and climbing plants suspend blossoms on such long stalks.

tree by building up their own trunks around it.

Others develop rosettes of overlapping leaves which catch and hold water; incidentally these also serve as breeding places for mosquitoes, frogs, and swarms of tiny invertebrates.

WORKERS AND WASTERS

Insect hordes swarm from the attic of the forest to deep beneath its floor. There are hundreds of thousands of varieties.

Here disguise is the highest art. There are "leaves" that hop, "flowers" that fly, and "bits of bark" that crawl. Butterflies may look like wasps, and caterpillars may appear as sinister as deadly spiders. By the wonderful process of variation, working through thousands of generations, all sorts of new body traits appear. And by the wonderful process of natural selection, any new trait that helps the species to survive tends to be passed on to later generations because it is those who have the trait that survive to have young.

The insects do vital work. Bees and others pollinate blossoms so that new plants can grow. Grasshoppers, termites, beetle grubs, and countless other insects chew up leaves, riddle trees, and destroy great quantities of growth. Termites break down glass-hard wood into spongy pulp. And army ants in their relentless march destroy all life that cannot flee.

An air tree (above) 35 feet high grows among small air plants on limb 120 feet up. Long roots reach to ground.

A gaudy butterfly alights for a moment on a leaf on the forest floor. Its bright colours may help to remind birds that its taste is bitter.

PAVILIONS IN THE SKY

It is mainly at night that the high-climbing animals clamber out from the shelter of the forest canopy to gather nuts and fruits. Day is a time of danger. When owls, eagles, falcons, and hawks patrol the skies, monkeys prefer the safety of their boudoirs in the canopy below.

The watch towers of the forest are left to the birds. During the long, hot day, clouds of swifts and other migrants wing past on their journeys to distant lands. Parrots and bright-feathered toucans preen themselves. And the tiny hummingbird poises on invisible wings above a nectar-filled flower opened toward the sun.

But at dusk the high climbers reappear—the squirrel monkeys, capuchins and red howlers outstanding among them. The squirrel monkey lacks a grasping tail, but he loves the heights and seldom goes below except to sleep or seek shelter from a storm. The capuchins (the organ-grinder type) do not even mind storms. Strong and hardy, they have become more numerous than any other South American monkey.

Most conspicuous of all, though, is the red howler, whose song is made up of the wildest, most ear-splitting and blood-curdling animal sounds on earth.

The howler owes his unmatched vocal powers to a hollow bone at the base of his tongue. This hollow has been enlarged and shaped through uncounted generations into an apple-sized sound chamber that makes his voice incredibly loud.

In the forest these howls can be heard for miles. From late afternoon through the night the challenges are made and answered at intervals as groups proclaim their territories. But toward morning they rise in volume into an almost continuous torrent of howls.

As the sky reddens with dawn, the monkeys quiet down under the scolding of the early-rising birds—the bad-tempered-sounding parrots and macaws, the umbrella birds, doves and toucanets.

And soon above appears the tyrant of the sky —the cruel-taloned harpy eagle with his 3-foot

wings outspread. When he swoops down, he rarely misses his prey, whether it is a leaping monkey or a stupid sloth. And overhead the jackal of the skies, the great king vulture, soars.

In the upper world of light a familiar figure is the king vulture (top left corner). Tree branches (left) hold two capuchin monkeys (lower left and upper right) and three squirrel monkeys. A gecko crawls up the trunk; in upper branches, doves perch. Two cloud swifts wing through the background. In front, a harpy eagle, claws ready, is about to alight. Below, half-hidden, are perched a red-tinged toucanet and an umbrella bird. Another squirrel monkey (top centre) seems to be complaining to a group of parrots. The three gay flyers at right are macaws, and the monkeys frolicking near them are red howlers.

PART XII

THE CHANGING WOODS

ADAPTING TO SEASONS

THE LOVELIEST of earth's adornments are the ever-changing woodlands with their yearly cycle of death and rebirth. These woods grow in the zones called temperate; but actually the climates are rather extreme. They have winter cold almost as bitter as in the Arctic, and summer heat almost as intense as in the tropics. It is this unusual rise and fall of the temperature that gives us the bursting buds of spring, the rich green leaves of summer, the gold and scarlet foliage of fall, and winter's bare boughs.

The dryness of winter is the greatest threat to the plants. For when the water is changed into ice it is not available for use. During the summer the trees and plants evaporate huge quantities of water from their broad leaf surfaces. In winter when this water is not available they simply drop their leaves and are as indifferent to lack of water as a desert cactus.

All through the winter they hibernate, "sleeping" until spring. Growth stops. Thick armour of bark around trunks and boughs, and tough scales around each tiny bud, protect them from bitter winter winds.

Trees and plants which drop their leaves are called deciduous, from the Latin *decidere*, meaning "to fall off." Almost all deciduous forests on earth lie in the Northern Hemisphere. South of the equator, the continental land masses taper off into the sea where these forests might have grown. But in the north they circle the globe as shown in the map below.

On the forest floor (at left) violets and skunk cabbage poke up through dead leaves in April. As the months pass, these leaves will disintegrate into soil.

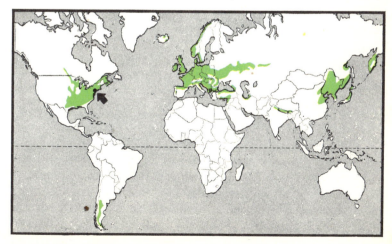

Deciduous forests of temperate zones are indicated in green. Our pictures are from the area shown by dot and arrow—a small New Jersey virgin forest known as Mettler's Woods.

The monarch oak rises straight and tall to the budding canopy of spring. At left its branches intertwine with those of a beech, and at right with branches of a black gum.

Skunk cabbage (below) unfolds broad purplish hoods to reveal tiny flower spikes. The familiar large, green, foul-smelling leaves appear later.

Today in the United States little untouched, or virgin, woodland remains. Of the 400,000 square miles encountered by the settlers of earlier days, only 1,600 square miles now remains, including the small New Jersey virgin forest known as Mettler's Woods, where these pictures were made.

To city folks, one woodland looks much like another. But there are really many different plant communities. Along the western edge of the American band of woodlands, where the rainfall edges down below 30 inches a year, oaks and hickories dominate. Along the Canadian border, deciduous (leaf-shedding) trees mingle with hardy conifers (cone-bearing trees) of the northlands. In American forests as a whole there are mainly oak, maple, beech, basswood, hickory, ash, and elm. But their combinations vary from place to place.

The canopy trees average 75 feet tall. Between them and the forest floor extends a band of low trees. In our pictured forest it is dogwood. Far below is the shrub layer—maple-leaved viburnum, spicebush, black haw, and arrow-wood. Clinging to the floor are the woodland herbs—May apple, spring beauty, violet, and anemone.

THE RUSH OF SPRING

In the still woods, spring rises from the forest floor. Late in March the frost melts in the soil and the little ground herbs stir. For they must flower before the canopy of tree leaves above shuts away the sun. Before the last snows melt, the green fingers of the skunk cabbage thrust up through the mud beside woodland streams. Their streaked, purplish hoods unfold to reveal spikes covered with tiny flowers to draw insects. Buds of May apple and spring beauty, and violet shoots also, appear.

Meanwhile within the trees secret changes are taking place. As the air and ground warm up, streams of sweet sap move upward to the tiny leaf buds wrapped in their scales. In response, the tiny leaflets within each bud begin to grow, forcing the scales apart. By mid-April the red maples are hung with ruby blooms, the cherry with white, the spicebush with yellow mist.

In May, spring comes with a rush, carpeting the earth with flowers—Solomon's seal, yellow bellwort, wild geranium. Overhead, white dogwood blossoms cloud the air. Viburnum gleams with white against its fresh green leaves.

Finally the tree leaves swell and burst—sugar maples, cherries, and beeches. The long, hairy catkins of the red oaks litter the ground. The candle-like buds on the hickory boughs explode in an emerald burst.

By mid-May the grand period of growth is at its peak. The hidden white flowers of the May apple are all but finished blossoming now. The oak leaves, last to come, weave their pattern in the thickening canopy overhead. And summer draws near in the changing woods.

Most woods animals are shy. Since man has cleared so much of their woodland, many of them have learned to hunt in fields and on farms. Like red and grey foxes they hunt by night.

At dusk an entire raccoon family may come

Jack-in-the-pulpit (below) is related to skunk cabbage. It has a flower-covered "club," hooded by a striped "pulpit."

Dwellers in the woods. At lower left a box turtle, a red-backed salamander, and a mole under a log. Just above, a red fox and cubs, and a tiny ring-necked snake. Above the deermouse (far left) a grey fox and a black racer snake; and on tree branches a pale mourning dove, opossum, crow, grey squirrel, downy wood-pecker. Below are chipmunk, raccoon and young, wood frog, and Fowler's toad (in the shadows). Right of

down from its tree home, looking for mice, frogs, or insects. The striped skunk and opossum also range by night. The opossum will eat anything from snakes to nuts. A great flesh-eater is the weasel. The tiny shrew will attack larger animals and can eat its own weight in flesh every day.

Insect-eating moles stay mostly underground.

Among the hunted, the vegetarians of the woods, are the largest woodland animals, the white-tailed deer. There are cottontail rabbits, deer mice, and woodchucks underground.

Some rodents live in the trees—the chipmunk,

centre, along the bottom, are striped skunk, black-and-white warbler, cottontail rabbit and young, and woodchuck in his hollow-tree doorway. Behind them are a white-tailed deer and fawns, with a tiny short-tailed shrew at heels of the fawns, a towhee on the grass, and a weasel on the branch eyeing the black-capped chickadee. At top, centre to right, a flying squirrel, male and female cardinals, and a scarlet tanager.

which feeds on the ground; the so-called flying squirrel, which glides supported by a membrane between its legs; and the alert, thrifty grey squirrel. And there are reptiles, too—the box turtle, the garter snake, the ring-necked snake, the speedy black racer. And there are amphibians —frogs and toads, and the red-backed salamander, which lays its eggs on land.

Among year-round bird residents are the handsome cardinal, the rowdy crow, the downy woodpecker, and the black-capped chickadee. In April the first migrants arrive, among them the

A woodland stream. At upper left is a spring peeper. Lower, in order, are green frog, fisher spider, horsefly larva, water flea (extreme left), cranefly larva, and two roundworms. Pink animal on leaf is a water mite; to its right, tubifex worms, mosquito larva (upper), and phantom larva (lower). Brown-marked frog at top is a pickerel frog; a little lower, a may fly. Frog on rock is a leopard frog. In zigzag order below it we see a shiner, sunfish, bullhead, water strider, and half-hidden horse leech. At top centre is a water snake. From

sweet-voiced song sparrow. Mourning dove, towhee, warblers, and gaudy scarlet tanagers soon follow. And by June the woodland echoes with song, while in countless nests lie the delicate eggs.

Spring floods bring fish and reptiles upstream from the rivers into the woodland brooks. Insects dance on the surface and many lay their eggs in the water—mayflies and damsel flies among them. Long-legged water striders, whirligig beetles, and others track the surface. Horseflies, crane flies, and fisher spiders live at the stream's edge, while the diving beetle goes below, carrying a bubble of oxygen under his wing covers.

Now the big pickerel feeds on sunfish and sil-

bottom centre up are a many-legged asellus, a little fingernail clam, a fairy shrimp, and (farther right) a pond snail. The big turtle is a snapper; just below are hairworms. Between the oak leaves a pickerel pokes his head toward two damselflies. To right of leaves is a whirligig beetle, then (lower) a mud turtle, a back swimmer (to left), a musk turtle, and (lower right corner) a worm leech. To the left of the large diving beetle are a two-lined salamander and (next to the asellus) a scud. All these are stream residents.

very shiners. Whiskered catfish and bullheads prowl the stream bed by night, taking insect larvae and fairy shrimp for prey. Permanent residents like the pond snail, leeches, and fingernail clam survive summer drought and winter chill by burrowing in the mud, as do worms. Harmless water snakes skim the surface at night. The big,

cross snapping turtle (up to 40 pounds) and smaller musk and mud turtles lurk on the bottom.

Now along the stream, choirs of frogs gather and croak their love songs into the night. The spring peeper, who inflates his throat like bubble gum, turns up in March. In April come deeper-voiced frogs and the two-lined salamander.

Agents of decay: white fungi, bacteria, protozoans.

THE FULLNESS OF SUMMER

Summer is serene in the woods. The excitement of spring has waned. At times, thunderstorms shatter the peace of the afternoons, but mostly the trees are motionless, the woodland quiet under its leafy roof.

By early June the spring carpet of blossoms has faded. A few shade-loving plants do bloom through July and August—enchanter's nightshade, white clusters of pokeweed, orange blooms of touch-me-not.

The trees are quietly preparing for the year to come. Fruits are ripening; trunks and branches thicken; glucose is stored in twigs, trunks, and roots for new spring growth; winter buds appear. Yet on a billion leaves, hungry mouths are biting away. On the oak trees gall blisters appear. Beetles infest the elms. Dry days shrivel some of the green leaves overhead. Long before the nights grow cool, the canopy begins to thin.

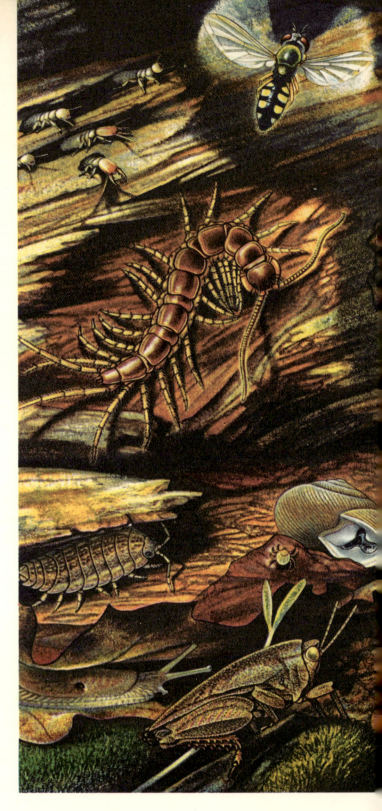

Down below, insect workers eat plants and chew into the heartwood of fallen trees. Fungi and bacteria labour in the soil. Termites tunnel into every fallen tree to devour the wood. The wood roach, too, passes its entire life beneath the bark of rotting trees, eating wood. The acrobat ant and the agile springtail also nest under bark.

Workers in the soil: At upper left, termites, a syrphus fly, and a centipede. At lower left are a sow bug and a slug (bottom). Beyond the grouse locust are a tick and a land snail. A bluish millepede is at bottom centre, with a mite to left and a partly concealed greenhead fly larva above. Larva of a fire-coloured beetle is on top of leaves. The butterflies are blues; to their right is a crane fly, and below is a yellowish wood roach. Lower still, safe under leaves, is a worm snake. Beneath it, curled next to tiny pseudoscorpion, is another millepede, and below this a 17-year cicada nymph. To right, little worms near ground snake are nematodes. On underside of log is a springtail. Near moth fly, lower right corner, we see an acrobat ant, big tiger beetle with an earthworm and a grass spider behind him, a firefly larva, a fungus gnat (upper right corner) and another centipede, just above which is a mottled, half-hidden slug. All do work in the soil.

Winged creatures of the woods here include (moving down from upper left) the underwing moth, stink bug, chrysalis of the swallowtail butterfly, and saddleback caterpillar. The big beetle is a fiery searcher. Above him is a wood nymph, and behind him a sphinx moth caterpillar with parasitic cocoons. At top centre is a lace bug; lower, eastern tent caterpillars; lower still. a potter wasp. The long-legged

Other scavengers of the forest floor include sow bug, mite, grouse locust, snail, slugs, nematodes, and millipedes. The tiny tunnellings of earthworms let air into the soil and also mix it, helping drainage and root growth.

Flying insects that stay close to the forest floor include blue butterfly, moth fly, syrphus fly, crane fly, and fungus gnat. Many, such as greenhead fly, firefly, and fire-coloured beetle, lay eggs in soil, and the larvae live there. The 17-year cicada stays below that long before adulthood!

Feeding on the worms, flies, and larvae are the

insect is a thalessa fly. A katydid stands on the leaf; oyster-shell scale shows on the twig beyond. At top left appears cottony maple scale. The big green moth is a luna moth. At extreme upper right is a golden-eyed lacewing; lower, a little green plant hopper. To left of the snow tree cricket (bottom right) is a marbled spider; farther left is a tree borer. The nightmarish caterpillar is called a "hickory horned devil."

brilliant tiger beetle, burrowing worm snake, prowling ground snake, grass spider, tick, and centipede. Some tunnel into soil and litter.

Flying insects outnumber all other visible forms of life. They even threaten man, eating his crops, infecting his animals, puncturing his skin.

High in the treetops, lace bug and plant hopper suck the juices of leaves.

Carpenter ants tunnel into the bark. Tree borers lay eggs there, and the larvae spread through the tree. Cottony maple scale and oyster-shell scale—legless, wingless—hold to the same

The monarch oak (seen also on page 180) in October holds its leaves to the last, among gold leaves of beech and scarlet ones of black gum.

Raccoon prepares himself for winter by feasting on insects. He will not hibernate, but takes long naps, living off fat.

branch all their lives, sucking sap. They often cover whole trees, killing them and infesting others nearby. Snowy tree crickets and katydids also chew leaves, as do moth and butterfly caterpillars. Tent caterpillars swarm out from their silken canopies in spring to strip huge areas of woods bare.

But for every leaf-eater there is a flesh-eater. The searcher beetle is out every night hunting caterpillars, pupae, grubs of all kinds. The potter wasp stings cankerworms and stores them, paralysed, in clay jars as food for its young.

The braconid wasp lays its egg under the skin of the sphinx caterpillar; the hatching larvae bore their way out and spin cocoons on the doomed caterpillar's back. Stinkbugs puncture

cocoons and suck the pupas' juices. Spiders trap all kinds of insects in their webs. Aphis lions gorge on plant lice, mites, and scales. So nature keeps a balance, and the green woods are kept green.

THE CLOSING YEAR

In mid-September, all living things in the woods seem to be waiting for some great change. In the still-soft evenings, streamers of mist gather above the stream bed. Trees, long before the first frost, manufacturing green chlorophyll. The emerald green of the leaves gives way to red and yellow. One by one the leaves turn, slowly at first, then swiftly during the brilliant days of October. Red maples are scarlet, beeches and hickories golden.

Autumn leaves drift to the forest floor. Here, against the fragments of a rotting hickory log, are maple leaves of faded rose, a few red dogwood leaves, and some tawny leaves of the sassafras.

At the base of each leaf stem, a layer of special thin-walled cells is formed. These are the separation cells, so fragile that at the touch of a breeze or a raindrop they give way, and the leaf falls.

During these golden days the animals prepare for winter too. They grow heavy winter coats of fur. And under those coats they build up layers of fat by eating as much as they can.

Raccoon noses under logs, searching for insects. Opossum eats everything he can find. Fox samples autumn's nuts and berries as a change from his diet of meat. Squirrels and chipmunks store thousands of nuts in their storerooms in hollow trees or underground.

The last migratory birds start southward, and the insect voices are stilled.

By November the forest floor is littered deep in rustling leaves. The hickories, elms, and maples are bare. Only the oak still wears a few leaves.

Opossum prepares for the lean days of winter by eating as much as she can hold during the autumn. In bad winter weather she may have to stay in her tree home for weeks.

It is a time of raw wind and dull skies. And on some nights frost touches the ground with white.

Soon, under the pale sun of winter, the forest is so silent it seems all life has fled. But even in deep winter there are signs of life. A breath of warm air from the south will bring out fresh shoots on the sedges, and patches of green moss.

All winter long there are footprints in the snow. The weasel and the fox go hunting even in the coldest weather. Rabbits, too are always about. Raccoon and skunk come out on milder days. And only ice on the trees keeps the squirrel inside.

Winter birds endure the cold by eating more than usual. Chickadees, woodpeckers, and nuthatches probe the bark for insect eggs and larvae.

Every night the crows gather noisily to roost.

Among the mammals in the woods, the chipmunk and the woodchuck hibernate, curled in snug burrows. The cold-blooded snakes and toads sleep the winter through under logs and leaf blankets. Frogs and turtles bury themselves in mud beneath the frozen streams. Insects sleep in trees, soil, or in silken cocoons.

So winter's quiet is the silence of sleep, not of death. Everywhere through the woods there is life—in the form of seeds, eggs, cocoons, buds, sleeping animals and plants. Each holds within itself the force of rebirth. And the animals too—the foxes, raccoons, and skunks—will mate during the winter to have new babies in the spring.

PART XIII

THE STARRY UNIVERSE

MAN'S VIEW OF SPACE

THROUGH THE ages, men of science have searched for knowledge about the world. This search has taken them to the depths of the seas and to the highest thin layers of the atmosphere, to deserts, jungles, and the frozen lands about the poles. As knowledge increased, man's views of time and space broadened. Each of the sciences has extended man's vision. But no other has been so humbling to him as astronomy.

Early man thought of himself as standing upon a firm, stationary earth, while above him the sun and moon wheeled regularly from east to west. The night sky seemed like a great rotating bowl studded with the bright diamonds of the stars.

Ancient astronomers, despite their mistaken views, did manage to chart the movements of many of the heavenly bodies. And they used these observations to figure out all our measurements of time. For all measurements of time depend on the sky and are actually measurements of movement in space.

An hour is an arc of 15° in the sun's apparent rotation. A day and night are the time the complete circle takes. A month is roughly the time it takes the moon to circle the earth.

As early as 3,000 B. C. the Egyptians worked out a calendar dividing the year into 12 months, or 365 days.

The Chinese kept records of eclipses of the sun as early as the 12th century B.C. Before 500 B.C. a Greek thinker, Pythagoras, decided the earth is a round sphere, and the stars much farther away than the sun and moon.

But for 2,000 years after that, men generally still thought the earth was the centre of the universe, with the sun revolving about it.

It was only in 1512 that Copernicus, a brilliant Polish scholar, began studies in which he decided that the earth was a "wanderer," revolving with other planets about the sun. In the next century Kepler traced the paths of the planets and found that they travelled in long loops called ellipses, not in circles.

After the invention of the telescope, about 1600, Galileo discovered many major features of the solar system—mountains of the moon, the phases of Venus, satellites of Jupiter, Saturn's rings, and sun spots. And through the centuries since, astronomers have continued the search ever deeper into space.

An eclipse of the sun seen in a multiple-exposure photograph. At left the sun rises, partly covered by the moon. As the golden ball moves higher, the moon covers more and more of it. For a few moments the moon is directly between earth and sun. Only the flaming corona of the sun is visible around the dark face of the moon. Then gradually the sun comes into view on the other side.

THE VASTNESS OF SPACE

During a clear night some 5,000 stars can be seen with the naked eye. A small telescope discloses over two million. And the great Palomar telescope picks up the light from billions. Yet the distances between them are so vast that the stars might be pictured as lonely lightships, a million miles apart (if the stars were as small as ships), floating in an empty sea.

The nearest star to the earth, save the sun, is Alpha Centauri, 4.4 light years away. (A light year is the distance light travels in a year at the rate of 186,000 miles a second—some six trillion miles.) The sun is only 8 light minutes away. Betelgeuse, the giant red star in the shoulder of Orion, is 650 light years away. The light from Rigel, the blue giant in Orion's knee, takes about the same time to reach our eyes.

Yet even these stars are close neighbours, and their distances are mere inches in the vast scale of the universe. We know now that our solar system is actually like a sprinkling of grains of sand far from the centre of the great galaxy of stars known as the Milky Way.

The Milky Way is only one unit in a cluster of galaxies, called the Local Group, which are linked together by gravitational pulls and which wheel together through space.

Astronomers reach the frontiers of vision two billion light years, or 12,000,000,000,000,000,000,000 terrestial miles, away. There even the physical laws of time and space break down. All our systems of measurement, our ordinary notions of form and shape, fail. We cannot fully understand a universe where space may have no end!

OUR NEIGHBOURS IN SPACE

The first careful watchers of the sky, beside the Rivers Nile and Euphrates, noticed that five bright "stars" changed their positions from night to night. The Greeks later named them "the wan-

The wastes of Mercury. The sun unendingly roasts the same side of this apparently airless planet. Because Mercury is much closer to the sun than Earth is, the sun in this painting looks two or three times as large as it looks from Earth. There is no weather—no wind or water—to erode Mercury's jagged, lifeless landscape.

The deserts of Mars. Mars has thin air and little moisture. Dust storms may have made the crescent dunes here. Rocks have been rounded by flaking due to sharp temperature changes between day and night.

derers." Today we know that they are not true stars burning in space like our sun. They are planets like the earth, circling the same sun and shining by its reflected light.

We know now that in addition to the five visible to the naked eye, there are three other planets which can be seen by telescope. Of the nine planets circling our sun, two are closer to it than Earth—tiny Mercury and bright, cloud-veiled Venus. Next comes Earth, with Mars beyond it, and then Jupiter. The outer planets are at vastly greater distances—Saturn, Uranus, Neptune, and Pluto (which, some now think, may be an escaped satellite of Neptune).

Because all these planets, like Earth, circle the sun and are lighted by it, men have often wondered if any of these neighbouring worlds might support life like our own.

Assuming that all the planets are made of the same elements as Earth and obey the same physi-cal laws, there could be no life like ours on the five outer planets. They are far too cold. Their surface temperatures range from −170°F. on Jupiter to −380° on distant Pluto. All save Pluto are also surrounded by dense clouds of poisonous gases.

The two innermost planets, Mercury and Venus, do not offer any friendlier setting for life as we know it. Mercury is airless, and it keeps the same face turned always toward the sun. On this side the temperature reaches 670°; on the other side the temperature is near absolute zero (−460°). Venus is surrounded by dense clouds containing much carbon dioxide. This gas is such a good insulator that the surface temperature of the planet may be close to that of boiling water—because the sun's heat cannot escape.

Except for Earth, only Mars among the planets seems likely to permit life. Mars is cold; its summer temperatures barely reach 50°. But Martian

197

The orbits of the planets. The picture above shows the paths of the inner planets, Mercury and Venus (both yellow), Earth (white), Mars (yellow), and Jupiter (green). Between Mars and Jupiter lies a belt of more than 30,000 asteroids (purple bands), the largest of which, Ceres (purple line), is only 480 miles in diameter. Encke's comet (the red oval at left) has a smaller orbit and shorter period (3.3 years) for its circuit than any other comet known. Below are orbits of the five outer planets (green), with Jupiter, the inner line, repeated for comparison with above. The planets, from centre, are Jupiter, Saturn, Uranus, Neptune, and Pluto. The red lines are comet orbits: Halley's, which appears every 77 years; and another, due back in four million years. Diagrams here show relative positions; space does not allow for scale.

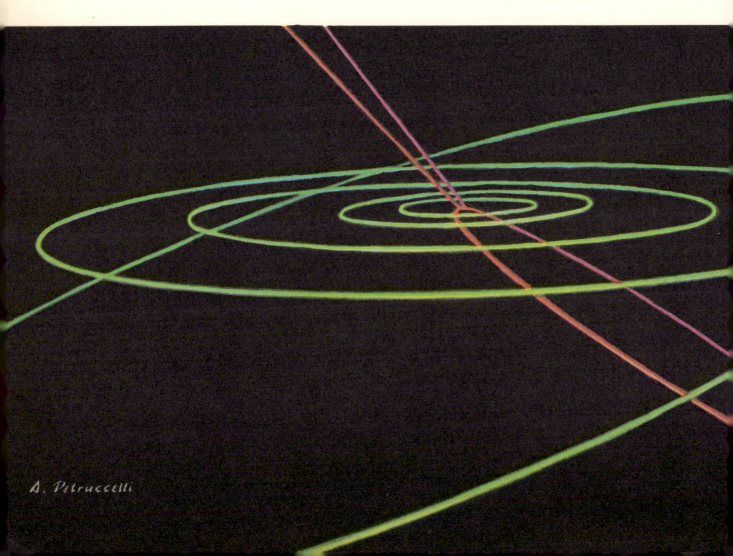

A. Petruccelli

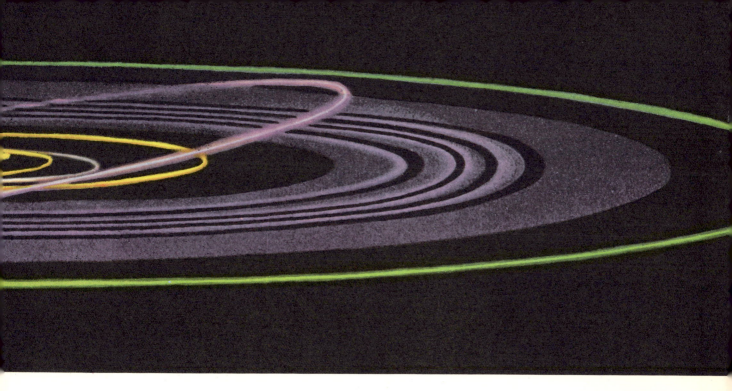

landscapes change colour with the seasons, showing brown in winter, **green** in summer. Possibly simple plant forms, such as lichens, do grow on Mars.

If higher forms of life exist elsewhere than on our earth, they must be found outside the solar system, in the starry spaces of the Milky Way or the distant galaxies beyond.

ORDER IN THE SOLAR SYSTEM

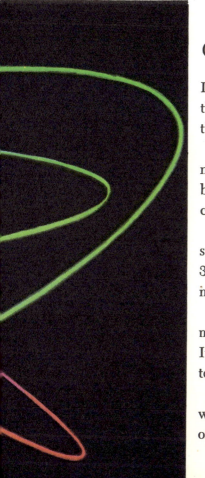

Looking out from Earth, we see the planets apparently wheeling across the heavens within a narrow belt of sky. The ancient star watchers called this belt the zodiac.

Today we know that the avenue of the zodiac is just our view of an enormous disc-shaped system in which our Earth and all the planets are held by the force of gravity. There they are all destined to revolve around our central star, the sun, as long as they exist.

Our solar system includes not only the nine planets but 31 moons or satellites of the planets (all shown in true scale on the pages following), 30,000 asteroids or minor planets, thousands of comets, and uncountable meteors, some of which vaporise in the earth's atmosphere every day.

The solar system is very complicated, but harmonious laws govern every motion within it. Each planet moves in an elliptical (oval) orbit or path. Its speed varies with its distance from the sun. It moves fastest when closest to the sun, more slowly when farther away.

A planet's movement represents a balance between two forces—inertia, which is a tendency to keep moving in a straight line, and gravity, the pull of the sun. This balance keeps each planet from flying off into space, on the

199

The solar system is pictured here with all its elements in scale. There is space to show only part of the rim of the enormous flaming sun. The nine planets and their 31 satellites are shown in the order of their distance from the sun. At far upper left float tiny Mercury and bright, pale Venus. Next comes blue-

one hand, or falling into the flaming mass of the sun, on the other.

The same laws rule the comets. As they reach the outer ends of their stretched-out orbits, the gravitational tug of the sun slows them and pulls them back. As they reach the inner end of their orbits, inertia and increasing speed carry them past the sun rather than into it.

To man on Earth, the dimensions of the solar system seem stupendous. Our small planet has a diameter of less than 8,000 miles, which seems large to us. But massive Jupiter is ten times this diameter, and the diameter of the sun is a hundred times that. It would take 1,300,000 building blocks the size of the Earth to make one sun—and the sun is only an average-size star. Earth is about

200

FOLD OUT—DO NOT TEAR——

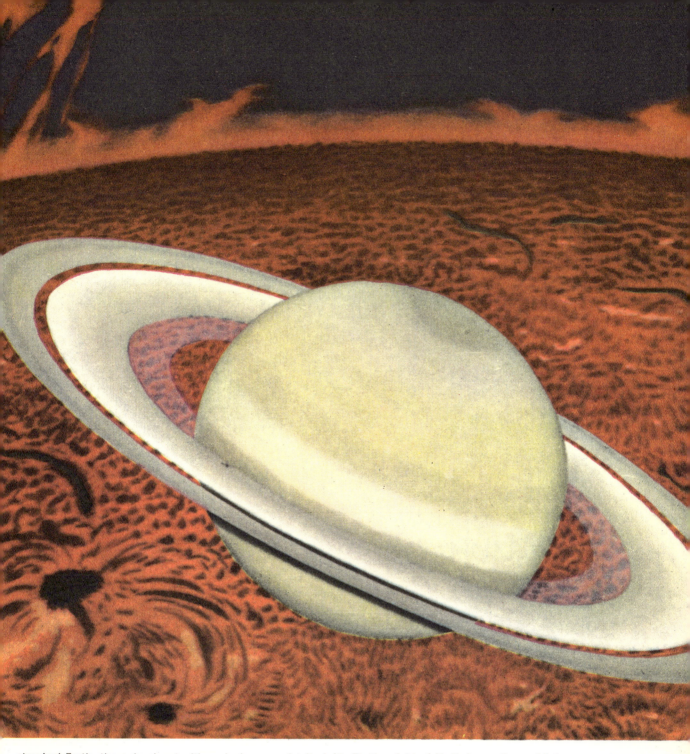

streaked Earth, the only planet with a single moon (at its left). To the right of Earth is smaller, reddish Mars with its two tiny satellites. Jupiter, 87,000 miles in diameter, has 10 of its 12 satellites strung out at its left, and another casting its shadow on the planet. (Actually the motions of these satellites around

93 million miles from the sun, and Pluto, the farthest planet, is nearly 40 times as far away. Yet even these distances seem petty to astronomers.

THE MILKY WAY

Let us imagine the sun as a ball 6 inches in diameter. Then the Earth, about 1/16 inch in diameter, would be about 55 feet away. Pluto, the outermost planet, would be about a half mile away. But the nearest stars would be about 3,000 miles away. And even these are near neighbours in the vastness of the Milky Way.

What we see in the sky as the Milky Way is only a part of the gigantic galaxy in which our solar system moves. The difficulty in picturing

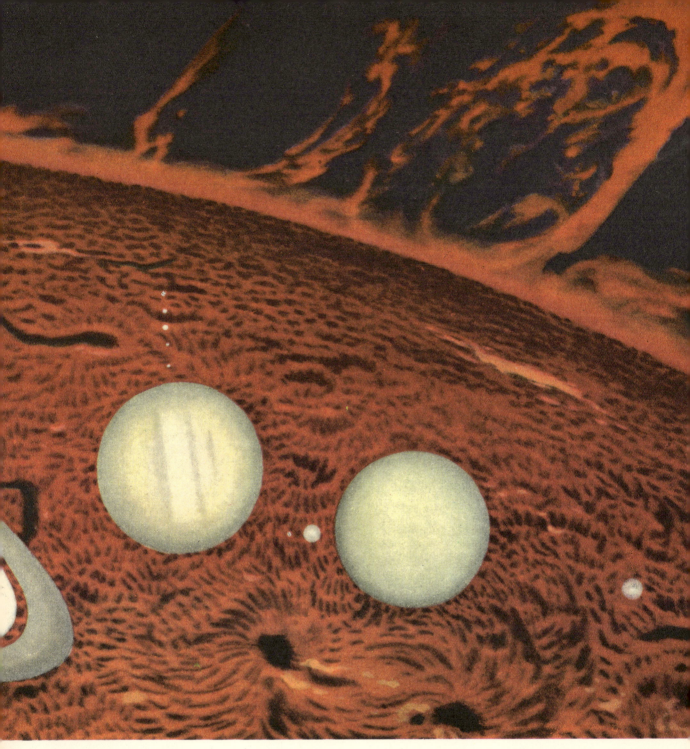

the planet are very intricate.) Saturn appears with its rings (consisting probably of countless tiny ice particles) and its nine satellites, one of which, Titan, is believed to have an atmosphere. The three outermost planets, discovered in recent times, are Uranus (1781), Neptune (1846), and distant Pluto (1930).

the structure of the Milky Way comes from the fact that we are inside it. (For a view from outside, see the following fold-out.)

We on Earth are situated some 30,000 light years from the centre of our galaxy. The over-all diameter of this one galaxy is 100,000 light years! It is an immense flattish disc, shaped something like a lens, with stars and dark clouds of gas and

dust scattered loosely through it. Most of the matter in our galaxy lies within the main disc of the Milky Way and its tightly coiled spiral arms.

The galaxy rotates. It completes one revolution every 250 million years and carries Earth and sun with it at about 600,000 miles an hour.

In its flight through space the main disc is accompanied by swarms of stars in the form of

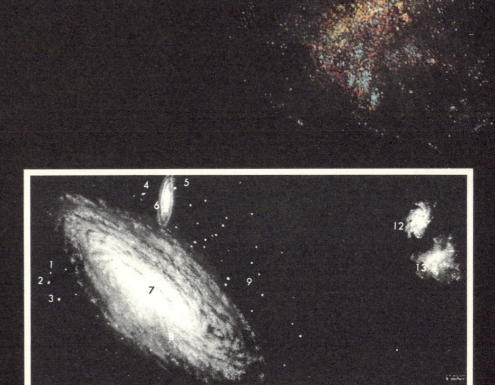

The Local Group of galaxies includes the Milky Way and 17 others. In the large picture the Milky Way (7 in the key) appears as if seen from 684,000 light years away. The sun's location is at 8. Globular clusters at the edges of our galaxy are at 9. At 6 is the Great Nebula in Andromeda, at far end of group and therefore looking relatively smaller than it really is. Other galaxies are 1, 2, 3, 4, 5, and 12. At 13 is a formless star system, one of two Magellanic Clouds, satellites of our galaxy about 150,000 light years away.

globular clusters, each revolving at random around the centre of the galaxy. Astronomers include these outer clusters when they speak of The Galaxy.

THE GALAXIES OF OUTER SPACE

Our galaxy is just one member of the still-larger unit called the Local Group. This includes 17 or more systems, all held loosely together by gravitational force within a radius of 15 million light years. Near one end of this vast super-system the Milky Way circles like a glowing wheel. At the other circles the great spiral sister galaxy, seen beyond the constellation Andromeda. Most of this huge local system—galaxies, globular clusters, and all—appears on pages 203-205.

But the eye of the telescope peers outward farther and farther. It gazes past the familiar constellations, the star patterns we see in the night sky. It sees the more distant star clouds and clusters of the Milky Way.

Far, far out it discovers more and more hazily glowing patches. These are the outer galaxies, the so-called "island universes." Each one is made up of billions of stars. But they are so vastly distant that their light takes many millions of years to reach Earth.

An elliptical galaxy in the Andromeda group, 1.7 million light years from Earth. The large stars visible in the foreground are in our Milky Way galaxy—approximately 100 to 100,000 times closer.

Look at the bowl of the Big Dipper. That rectangle covers only 1/2000th of the whole sky. But within it, powerful telescopes can pick up faint glimmers of light from a cluster of 300 galaxies or more. By comparison our Local Group with its 17 members is a dwarf cluster.

The outer galaxies tend to group together in communities of about 500, united by gravity. Often in their wanderings they collide. About a trillion galaxies lie within the range of our largest telescopes. Of those observed 17 percent are elliptical, 80 percent spiral, and 3 percent irregular, like the formless Magellanic Clouds. Some elliptical galaxies are saucer-like in shape, while spirals may be tightly coiled or have long, loose pinwheel arms. The irregulars have no pattern of motion; spirals are fast-spinning, the ellipticals slower. Probably all the galaxies were created at about the same time.

THE COSMIC CLOUDS AND CREATION

Drifting in outer space as clouds of gas and dust is a great deal of matter. We see these clouds

Cosmic gas clouds (below) are caused to glow by radiation from nearby stars. Star in centre is overexposed.

Purple Pleione, one of the seven sisters of the Pleiades, rotates so fast that it has flattened out somewhat. Around it is a red ring of hydrogen, partly hiding the violet star.

when they catch the light of nearby stars. They average only 16 atoms per cubic inch—fewer than in the most perfectly empty vacuum men can produce on earth. Yet in some regions these clouds are so vast that they equal in mass the atoms in the nearby stars.

Cosmic clouds are important because they may be like the raw material from which our world was created. Some five billion years ago our galaxy probably consisted of swirling clouds of hydro-

gen gas rotating in starless space. As the clouds spun, eddies formed in them. In those eddies, gravity began to lump particles of matter together into larger bodies. As these masses became more compressed by gravity, their internal temperatures rose. Eventually, in the hot centre of each mass, atomic nuclei began to break up as they do in an H-bomb. Hydrogen was changed to helium, and energy set free by the process lit up these first stars. In this way perhaps all the galaxies formed.

Among the immense, dim clouds in the depths of the sky, this same slow process may be going on still. A few astronomers believe new matter is still actually being created in the vast spaces between the galaxies. But most believe all the matter in the universe was created at one time.

How long ago was that?

Most astronomers now say, "About 5 billion years." At least three kinds of evidence point to this figure: first, radioactivity in the earth's crust; second, the time it has taken (as indicated by

Spiral arms of galaxies shine with the brilliance of many young blue stars of Population I. These are on the rim of the Great Nebula in Andromeda, which is a twin galaxy of our Milky Way. This section of the galaxy, 1/30 of the total, is about 11,000 light years across.

A **stellar explosion** left this enormous gas cloud, known as the Crab Nebula. Chinese astronomers in A.D. 1054 observed a nova in this location. The cloud is 3¼ light years wide and is still expanding at 684 miles per second.

star colours and other data) for light from distant galaxies to reach the earth; and third, the rates of expansion of inner and outer parts of the universe (see page 211).

CLASSIFYING THE STARS

Seen through the telescope, the silvery stars turn into jewels of every colour known. Since the glow of a star is from heat, its colour depends on its temperature. Red stars are relatively cool, with surface temperatures of about 6,000°F. Yellow stars, like our sun, are hotter by thousands of degrees, and blue stars are still hotter. The hottest ultraviolet stars may be 100,000°.

Relationships exist between the colour and size of stars and their age and location in the galaxies. Stars tend to fall into two great categories called Population I and Population II. Population I consists of stars in the arms of spiral galaxies and in irregular galaxies like the Magellanic Clouds. Population II consists of stars in the nuclei of spiral galaxies, in elliptical galaxies, and in globular clusters.

The biggest, brightest stars in Population I are blue giants, which spread a blue radiance around them. The biggest, brightest stars of Population II are red giants, which give their surroundings a reddish-orange tint.

In Population I, the smaller stars are red and relatively cool — that is, cool for stars. The larger ones are blue and hot. Until a few decades ago, astronomers believed that the bigger stars are, the hotter they are. Then, as telescopes probed deeper into space, new populations of stars were found. Out in remote globular clusters and still more distant galaxies, the giant stars were red and cool. And even in our own galaxy some stars have been discovered that change periodically in size and brightness. These are the so-called pulsating, or variable, stars. Some change regularly; some are irregular.

As nuclear physics developed, astronomers learned more about processes that go on in the

Double stars are common. More than three quarters of the stars in our galaxy travel in groups of two or more, or in clusters, with a common centre of gravity. Here a large dim red star and a smaller bright blue one travel in the same envelope of gas and revolve about each other. They are casting two-toned shadows on a hypothetical planet.

stars. Then it became clear that different types of stars represent different stages in star evolution. Apparently Population I stars are in earlier stages of their evolution, and Population II stars are probably in later stages.

THE LIFE AND DEATH OF THE STARS

The life of a star generally develops like this:

1. At first it burns steadily, without much change in character. Big stars burn more rapidly than small ones. This goes on until about 15 percent of the hydrogen has been burned. (We say "burn" just for convenience; actually what happens is not the usual kind of burning, which is oxidation.)

2. After a star has used up 15 percent of its hydrogen, it begins to cool and expand, swelling to 50 or 100 times its original size. It becomes a red giant or super giant with as much as eight billion times the volume of the sun. Now it spends its fuel swiftly, consuming the remaining 85 percent as quickly as the first 15 percent.

3. When 60 percent of its hydrogen has been used up, the star's internal pressures begin to fall. Its swollen exterior caves in. As it contracts it may pulsate for a while. Or it may flare up violently as a nova.

4. Finally the star collapses and becomes a white dwarf. It glows only by the feeble heat of slow compression. Its substance is squeezed together until every cubic inch may weigh several tons.

Apparently, new blue giants are always being formed to replace stars that burn out. For the spiral arms of galaxies contain great quantities of dust and gas for the formation of new stars—which globular clusters lack.

So we always see the Milky Way burning with youthful blue brilliance. Really it already has many more small red and yellow stars than blue giants. Eventually its cosmic clouds will be used

A globular cluster, one of many at the edges of the Milky Way, glows with the light of a million stars. All stars in such clusters are probably old. Toward the cluster's centre they are packed more densely. The cluster is about 245 light years in diameter.

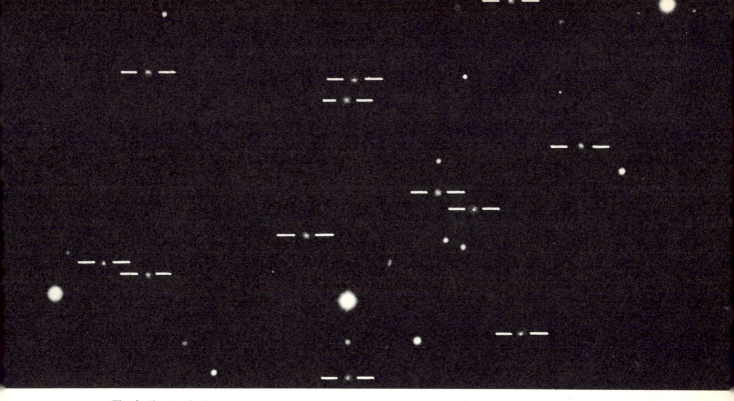

The farthest galaxies that man can see are indicated by lines in this photo taken by the 200-inch Palomar telescope. An hour's exposure was needed to capture their faint light, which has been travelling toward us for 2 billion years or more. The brighter objects are nearer galaxies and stars in our Milky Way.

up. No more new stars will be formed. Its blue giants will have faded. And the light from the galaxy will grow faint and yellow. But 50 billion years may pass before the last faint star flickers out into everlasting night.

THE EXPANDING UNIVERSE

The universe appears to be expanding in all directions. Think of it as a balloon covered with bright solid dots for the galaxies. As the balloon is blown up, each spot moves farther away from every other spot. So every galaxy is rushing away from every other. The outermost travel fastest, at speeds up to 120,000 miles per second. When their light reaches us, the galaxies are far from the spot where we see their light.

Counting back, it seems probable that they all started from the same place at the same time, some five billion years ago. New stars may even now be forming from raw material in the galaxies. But the clues of science—geology as well as astronomy—tend to point to the same time of creation of the universe—about five billion years ago.

A cosmic "smoke ring" surrounds a faint star in the constellation of Aquarius. This is actually a shell of gas caused to glow by the light of the star.

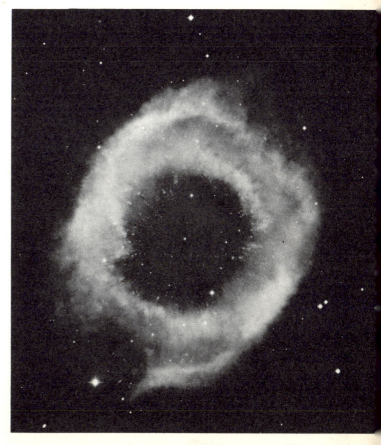

PICTURE CREDITS

INDEX

Subjects that have two or more words are often listed under the main word. For example, to find "ladder monkey" look up "Monkey." **Heavy type** refers to an illustration of the subject.

216

PRINTED BY INTERDRUCK LEIPZIG
GDR 1970

The double star Beta Lyrae is pictured here as it might be seen from an imaginary nearby planet. It is one of the numerous stars that are known to consist of two or more members. Part of the glowing hydrogen cast off by the rapidly spinning blue member is attracted and held by the smaller yellow member; the rest escapes into space in an ever-widening spiral.

Chesley Bonestell